THE RESEARCH PAPER AND THE WORLD WIDE WEB

Dawn Rodrigues

University of Texas at Brownsville /
Texas Southmost College

PRENTICE HALL
Upper Saddle River, NJ 07458

Library of Congress Cataloging-in-Publication Data

Rodrigues, Dawn.
    The research paper and the World Wide Web / Dawn Rodrigues.
      p.   cm.
    Includes bibliographical references and index.
    ISBN 0-13-461724-X
    1. Report writing—Data processing.   2. Research—Data processing.
   3. World Wide Web (Information retrieval system)   4. Internet
(Computer network) in education. I. Title.
    LB2369.R585   1997
    808'.02—dc21   96-48356
                                                          CIP

Editorial Director: Charlyce Jones Owen
Executive Editor: Mary Jo Southern
Assistant Development Editor: Kara Hado
Director of Production and Manufacturing: Barbara Kittle
Project Manager: Maureen Richardson
Manufacturing Manager: Nick Sklitsis
Prepress and Manufacturing Buyer: Mary Ann Gloriande
Interior Design: Alison Gnerre
Cover Director: Jayne Conte
Marketing Manager: Rob Mejia
Copyeditor: Lynn Buckingham
Proofreader: Marjorie Shustak

This book was set in 10/12 New Century Schoolbook by A & A Publishing Services, Inc.
and was printed and bound by Courier Companies, Inc. The cover was printed by
Phoenix Color Corp.

© 1997 by Prentice-Hall, Inc.
Simon & Schuster/A Viacom Company
Upper Saddle River, NJ 07458

Netscape Communications Corporation has not authorized, sponsored, or endorsed,
or approved this publication and is not responsible for its content. Netscape and the
Netscape Communications Corporate Logos, are trademarks and trade names of
Netscape Communications Corporation. All other product names and/or logos are
trademarks of their respective owners.

Printed in the United States of America
10 9 8 7 6 5 4 3 2 1

ISBN 0-13-461724-X

Prentice-Hall International (UK) Limited, London
Prentice-Hall of Australia Pty. Limited, Sydney
Prentice-Hall Canada Inc., Toronto
Prentice-Hall Hispanoamericana, S.A., Mexico
Prentice-Hall of India Private Limited, New Delhi
Prentice-Hall of Japan, Inc., Tokyo
Simon & Schuster Asia Pte. Ltd., Singapore
Editora Prentice-Hall do Brasil, Ltda., Rio de Janeiro

CONTENTS

PREFACE

As a student or a professional involved in writing research reports, you have probably begun to use technology as a tool for information gathering. You may have used online catalogs, CD-ROM databases, and other computer resources available to you in libraries on campus or in your community. And you may have begun to incorporate the Internet and the World Wide Web into your search processes. But chances are you've got some unanswered questions about such things as library sources available on the Web, proper citation of Internet sources, or more specific topics such as accessing an Internet or Web site.

If you are a student, the knowledge of online and Internet searching presented here will help you in other courses. The basic research techniques presented here should help you conduct research in your major. If you are working in business or industry, you'll be able to develop information-gathering skills that will apply to your job.

This book will attempt to clarify the interplay between traditional text sources, electronic sources, and Web sources in your research process. It will (1) demonstrate how to use Web tools to search the Web and to search libraries on the Internet, (2) provide you with starting points for finding local and worldwide resources on the Internet, and (3) suggest ways you can organize all the information you find.

In the first chapter you will review the basics of searching both the library and the World Wide Web. Later, you will learn how to link traditional library searching with Internet searching and how to incorporate citations for online sources into your drafts. You may be surprised to find that you can do the bulk of your research without setting foot in the library.

This is not to denigrate the importance of the library as a place to find information; the serendipitous finding of a great source on the shelf next to the source you have identified is something that doesn't always happen quite as easily on the Internet. But as libraries make their collections accessible online world, they allow people everywhere to have the advantages that only the few who lived close enough to major university libraries have had in the past.

THE HOME PAGE
FOR THIS BOOK

This text has its own home page on the Web at http://www.prenhall.com/rodrigues. Visit this page as soon as possible. There you will find links to all Web sources mentioned in this book as well as chapter updates, review questions, and chat areas where students and others using this text in different parts of the country can collaborate on information gathering for research projects. You will also find a list of documents related to the writing suggestions at the end of each chapter. These sources can be used as starting points for research on the topics.

The Web page and accompanying activities promise to make this book dynamic rather than static. Readers can interact with the author and with other readers—discussing ideas, debating issues, critiquing the chapters—thereby making the text a living book. You can collaborate with peers at other schools or companies as you conduct your research. For example, you might consider developing an annotated bibliography together; you could discuss concepts related to your projects; or you could review drafts of one another's work. You can join one of several discussions that will be moderated by the author or you can contribute to an ever-expanding list of resources for research that will be maintained by the author. We hope the Web site will become a medium of exchange for readers as well as an electronic repository and distribution point for supplementary information and insights about research and writing.

ACKNOWLEDGMENTS

I would like to thank the reviewers, Michael Freeman, Utah Valley State College; Michael Day, South Dakota School of Mines and Technology; Margaret-Rose Marek, Texas Christian University; Marcia Peoples Halio, University of Delaware, for their numerous helpful suggestions.

First, I want to thank my husband, Ray, and my son, Brad, for their encouragement and advice. I couldn't have completed a task like this without their support. Next, I'd like to say how much I appreciated the supportive and warm working relationship I've had with my editors at Prentice Hall: Alison Reeves, Mary Jo Southern, Kara Hado, and Maureen Richardson.

INTRODUCTION: HOW THIS BOOK IS ORGANIZED

Chapter 1, "The Research Process in the Information Age," provides an overview of the research and writing process, giving a sense of how Web searching can be integrated with library research. Chapter 2, "A Researcher's Introduction to the Web," gives an understanding of what the Web offers and how it developed. Chapter 3, "The Basics of Web Navigation," explains how to find resources for your research on the Web and how to create bookmarks that enable you to mark selected sites for later retrieval. Chapter 4, "Finding Libraries on the Web," tells how to locate libraries throughout the world on the Internet. Chapter 5, "Finding Library Resources on the Web," offers a sense of what is in the library and what is on the Web. This chapter points to the many standard library resources available at Web sites and also directs the reader to complementary Internet resources.

Chapter 6, "Finding Resources in the Disciplines," introduces subject catalogs on the Web with worldwide links to sites for research in different disciplines. Chapter 7, "E-mail, Mailing Lists, and Newsgroups as Research Tools," helps readers learn about additional ways to gather information for Internet-intensive research projects. Chapter 8, "Organizing Research Notes and Sources," gives guidance on organizing a range of data, including notes from books and Web pages. Readers will learn new ways of storing e-mail notes they have captured while conducting online library searches. Chapter 9, "Documenting Sources," reviews traditional citation format and teaches ways to cite Internet sources.

CHAPTER 1

THE RESEARCH PROCESS IN THE INFORMATION AGE

You are probably already familiar with using the library for research. But because technology has been advancing so rapidly and has made it possible for writers to access sources electronically, you need to begin thinking about research in new ways. In particular, you should see research as a process which includes both print and online sources. This chapter will provide you with an overview of how to search, take notes, and start writing your research paper by integrating print and online sources.

RESEARCH IN THE INFORMATION AGE

Writing a research paper or report used to mean spending hours on end in a library, wading through card catalogs—electronic or paper-based—and taking notes from the books and journals available. With vast resources of information having moved outside library walls and onto the Internet and the World Wide Web, research and writing processes are changing. Clearly, research that excludes the Internet and the Web and other online sources is not comprehensive research. Not only library collections, but also databases on topics across disciplines are available on the Web. Web sources on your topic should not be overlooked as you collect information for your research project.

Before the Web was a reality, students were limited to the sources available in their own library or to the books they might reasonably expect to get through interlibrary loan. The topics students could select for research were, as a result, limited somewhat by the physical library collection. If, for example, you wanted to do a research paper on the Holocaust but discovered that your library had only a few books and journals available, you might not have chosen to stay with this topic. But with the

Web and CD-ROM databases available to you, you have access to many libraries' resources on your topic as well as to new kinds of information that have been developed and made available outside the boundaries of the library. You can access a Holocaust site such as the Holocaust Studies Center (http://www.bxscience.edu/orgs/holocaust/home.html); or for a research paper on the Civil War, you can access digitized photographs and diaries from the Library of Congress's collection of American photographs and film strips (http://www.loc.gov).

The Web offers other new possibilities. You can quote from mailing list discussions or take notes from Web pages, or you can supplement or replace face-to-face interviews and surveys with online equivalents.

If you happen to use the Web extensively as you search for information, your research process is likely to change. In the dynamic environment of the Web, research is often a dialogical process: you interact with others, and your interactions change you. A reference that you find by using a search tool such as WebCrawler (see chapter 3), a note from a colleague on e-mail, or a response to a posting on a newsgroup might cause you to reexamine your topic or to think of new angles for investigation (see chapter 7 for a discussion of e-mail and newsgroups).

THE RESEARCH AND WRITING PROCESS

This chapter provides you with some suggestions for moving through the research process and offers advice for integrating library and Web searching throughout your research and writing processes. You will find more detailed advice on some topics in later chapters. You can also find assistance on writing research papers online at sites such as the following:

- Cornell Library "Library Research: A Hypertext Guide"

  http://urisref.library.cornell.edu

  How to prepare an annotated bibliography; a list of class-related bibliographies; guides on how to conduct research from choosing a topic to limiting search terms to citing sources.
- University of Illinois Writer's Workshop On-Line Handbook

  gopher://gopher.uiuc.edu/11/Libraries/writers

  Guide to information on bibliographic style in MLA (Modern Language Association), APA (American Psychological Association), and Old-MLA formats (footnote style).

ESTABLISH A TOPIC
OR RESEARCH PROJECT
BY READING AND SEARCHING

Don't begin by finding a topic or selecting a research project at random. Rather, begin by thinking about a range of possibilities and delaying your selection of a specific topic or project until after you've done preliminary searching and reading.

Your research projects should be meaningful to you personally, whether they are assigned by teachers or self-generated. If you select topics that you *want* to investigate critically and subjects you have a need to explore in depth, then you are certain to benefit from the research process. If you customize and personalize assigned topics, you will enjoy your research. If you incorporate the Web into your research process, you will have the added satisfaction of developing an important information-age skill.

You can find your own topic or refine one assigned to you in many ways. You can begin reading some general sources, you can search for Web sources, you can talk with your friends face-to-face, or you can chat with people from around the world in online chat areas. In *Searching Writing,* Ken Macrorie says that it is much better to let a topic "find you" than to settle on a topic just because you have to write a paper (1980).

A topic is more likely to "find you" if you are not in a hurry. A great time to "surf" the net for general information on your subject area is *before* you've settled on a specific focal point for your research. Web browsing and searching can help you generate possibilities if you relax and let your mind roam. Time is a factor, of course. If you have a project due in a few days, you don't have the luxury of a freewheeling search for ideas.

You can, however, allow topic possibilities to percolate in the back of your mind while you do preliminary reading if you do have time to spare. As you search for information and skim available sources, you will gradually gain a sense of what interests you and you will develop a sense of what has been said about your topic by others.

Here are some questions to guide you as you explore topic possibilities:

- Do I have a choice of topics or research areas? What are the restrictions on my topic? What is the range of possibilities?
- Is this an Internet-intensive kind of project?
- Are there any Web areas that I might use to help me identify a topic or project? What Web areas would be particularly useful for my field of study?
- What aspects of my potential research project are most intriguing to me?
- What standard library sources should I consult?

- What CD-ROMs does my library have that I should explore?
- What are the most obvious approaches to my topic or area of investigation? How can I find out?
- What am I most interested in learning about?

PRACTICE BOX

1. What are some topics or project areas that you care about? Who else that you know might want to talk about these topics, too? If you have free choice of topic, think of issues that are receiving attention in the press. Ask if anyone is interested in researching the same topic with you. You will be able to explore online news sources more productively if you work with a partner.

2. Visit your library. Learn how to access the online card catalog. Find out if it is available on the Web. Examine the CD-ROM databases available to you. Find out if they are available on the Web. Find out whether you have online access to the full text of journals. Search the online card catalog and the databases using a working topic.

3. If you are working on a research paper or project for a writing-intensive course in a specific discipline, find out what kinds of topics are acceptable in your field. Examine sample papers to learn about ways researchers present the results of their work. (See chapter 8 for ideas.)

4. Do a library search on several related topics using the online catalog in your library. Even if you get good results on the first search, try searching with a few different terms just to get a sense of possibilities. Save or print search results.

If you already have Internet or Web expertise:

1. Send your group members or your teacher an e-mail note telling what you have decided to write about and indicating to what extent online searching may have influenced your selection of topics.

2. If you already know how to access the website for this book, try posting to the chat area at the end of chapter 1 (http://www.prenhall.com/rodrigues).

3. If your local library is accessible from the Web, explore its holdings directly through the Web page.

Establish Research Questions

Research is the exploration and investigation of a question or a set of questions you want to know more about. You will take your work more seriously if you first formulate research questions, whether the research is an exploration of affirmative action issues, a look at current debates about copyright issues on the Web, a complex scientific experiment, or an exploration of technology use in schools and colleges.

Whether you are using the Web as a key tool or as merely a part of your research process, you need to go through the same basic steps researchers have gone through for ages. You need to begin by establishing research questions to help clarify your topic and to direct your research process. Taking time to select and identify a research question helps turn even a dull writing assignment or research project into an exciting one. The following box includes some suggestions for how you can develop research questions.

Developing Research Questions

1. State your topic as a question.

Examples:

Topic: Technology in Colleges and Universities
Question: "What are the most cost-effective ways to incorporate technology into college instruction?"

Topic: Affirmative Action
Question: "Why is affirmative action a contested issue?"

2. Pose several sub-questions.

Examples:

Topic: Technology in Colleges and Universities
Subquestions:

"What kinds of opposition to technology use can be expected from students?"
"What opposition to technology integration can be expected from faculty?"
"Can effective use of the Internet solve some of those problems?"
"What methods of integrating technology into teaching are most effective nationally? locally?"

Topic: Affirmative Action
Subquestions:

"What are the positive and/or negative effects of recent affirmative action policies?"
"What different reactions have Latinos, African Americans, and Asians had to affirmative action policies?"

"Why has legislation turned against affirmative action?"
"Is it possible to overturn recent legislation that has turned against affirmative action?"
"How does recent legislation affect colleges?"

Sample Research Questions.   Below are some samples of good research questions on several topics, including "technology in the schools" and "affirmative action." Under each item are some suggested research strategies.

1. **Will recent changes in affirmative action policies affect diversity on college campuses?** Find out what the racial and/or ethnic mix of students is on your campus. What would change if affirmative action were no longer allowed? Consider how affirmative action policies evolved on your campus and nationally. Find out why they evolved as they did. See what problems exist on your campus. Find out what students, faculty, and administrators think needs to be done.
   Possible strategies for answering preliminary questions:
   -Interview key personnel on your campus.
   -Locate and read campus policies on affirmative action. (See if they are archived on your campus Web page.)
   -Search your library catalog for possible sources.
   -Search government documents for policy sheets.
   -Use Web search tools to do a Web search.
   -Join an affirmative action listserv.

2. **To what extent is technology changing instruction on campuses across the country?** What is driving the use of technology: a desire to improve instruction or a dream of saving money? Are students satisfied with their access to computers on your campus? How does your campus compare to other campuses with regard to technology use? Are students encouraged to create their own home pages? Do students on your campus who come from schools with high-tech environments have a decided advantage over other students? What kinds of computer experiences should students have in college? What are the economic factors that a school or college must consider before expanding technology resources?
   Possible strategies for answering preliminary questions:
   -Interview professors who use technology in teaching.
   -Interview students who have taken computer-intensive courses.
   -Find out if your college or university offers distance learning. If so, learn as much as you can about how the courses are conducted.
   -Read different articles presenting different views of the technology integration topic and note what the key questions seem to be. (*Educom Review* [http://www.educom.com]; *Syllabus* [http://syllabus.com])

-Join the American Association of Higher Education's discussion list on technology to tune in to the kinds of issues that are of interest to administrators and professors.

-Use e-mail to interview students at different schools.

Develop Research Processes

With your topic under control and research questions identified, take time to develop comprehensive research processes. Your approach should include such activities as: (1) planning a research agenda (e.g., library searching, surveys, interviews, experiments); (2) selecting search tools and organizational strategies; (3) identifying keywords; (4) developing a system for note taking and organizing sources; (5) preparing a working bibliography; (6) continuing your search and reevaluating your research plans; (7) validating your sources; (8) drafting, revising, and editing your paper.

1. PLANNING A RESEARCH AGENDA.   After you have established your research questions, you will be in a better position to determine what research methods are appropriate to your topic. You may need to combine library searching with interviewing, conducting experiments, developing surveys, or observing behavior in research sites. In all cases, however, you will need to do at least some library and Web searching to learn more about your topic and to gain a working knowledge of what others think about your topic or what research they have conducted in the general area.

Some of your research strategies will be driven by the expectations of your field. Even if you are in a freshman-level course, you may want to learn more about the expectations that professors in specific disciplines would have for a paper on your topic. If, for example, your paper is on affirmative action, you can learn how sociologists conduct and report research. If you wish to, you can build learning about research in a specific discipline into your research agenda. Not only will you have gained expertise about a specific topic, but you also will have oriented yourself to the conventions and ways of thinking that are characteristic of your discipline. (See chapter 6 for guidance on tailoring research to specific disciplines.)

2. SELECTING SEARCH TOOLS AND ORGANIZATIONAL STRATEGIES.   After doing some preliminary browsing and searching, decide which Web search tools and references you will use for the balance of your research and which library catalogs you plan to explore. In addition, think about how you'll organize your search results. (See chapter 3 for a discussion of search tools. Chapter 8 explains how to use bookmarks and file structures to organize your notes.)

3. IDENTIFYING KEYWORDS. Develop a list of keywords or "descriptors"—words that describe your topic and that are likely to have been used

in titles or abstracts of the books and journals you are exploring. Continually revise this list. It is a good idea to search a variety of databases using the same terms, expanding your list of keywords as you find new keywords or "cross-references." When the database you are searching suggests that you "see also" several other topics, take note of these words and sources and see what kinds of results you get when you change search terms.

Identifying Keywords

Topic: Technology in Colleges and Universities
Keywords: technology, computers, colleges, universities
Keyword Combinations: technology and college; teaching, technology, teaching and universities; technology and university teaching
Concepts: Technology integration, computers in the curriculum, computer-mediated instruction

Topic: Affirmative Action
Keywords: affirmative action, racism, quotas
Keyword Combinations: affirmative action and college or university, affirmative action and Latino, affirmative action and African American, affirmative action and Asian
Concepts: hiring practices, affirmative action policies

If you begin your research with library card catalogs, you should consult the Library of Congress Guide to Subject Headings to help you develop your list of keywords. Libraries use a standard set of terms to categorize their holdings. The Library of Congress Subject Headings, bound volumes containing lists of these terms, are usually located near a library's reference desk. An online method of finding correct headings is to find one book or journal on your topic by doing either an author or a title search. When you display the full record, you can see what subject headings have been assigned to your topic.

If you begin your research on the Web, you will need to use keywords that correspond to main concepts or to topics that you would expect to find in your sources. Unlike the Library of Congress, the Web uses no standardized set of keywords; nonetheless, you can use many of the same keywords for both library and Web searching. If you start your search with the Web, try using the words that come naturally to you when you talk about a given topic.

After you see your results, you'll know whether you need to narrow or broaden your search. In many library catalogs and on most Web sites, you can do some Boolean searching, which allows you to use AND, OR, and NOT to define the conditions of your search. (Note: George Boole was an English mathematician who developed ways of describing the contents of mathematical sets by using AND, OR, and NOT.) If you search for information on affirmative action using Boolean operators, you would be able to search in the following ways:

- **affirmative OR action**—This combination would give you all the information that uses the term *affirmative* or the term *action;* this would not be a good idea. You typically use OR with synonyms or related concepts, as in the next example.
- **affirmative action OR diversity**—This list of words would give you all the information that uses the term *affirmative action* along with the information that uses the term *diversity.* You are likely to get a large list of information. (When you put two words together without an AND, most search tools use AND as the default.) It's often a good idea to use OR early in your searching when you want to look at a broad sample of what is available on your topic. *Use OR to broaden your search.*
- **affirmative action AND diversity**—These search directions would provide you with all the sources that use both *affirmative action* and *diversity.* This would limit your search. You'd only get the information that happened to use both terms. If you want to focus on the implications of affirmative action on understanding racism and diversity issues, this would be a good choice.
- **affirmative action AND class**—This strategy would provide you with only those sources about affirmative action that mention something about class issues. This is a good strategy to use when you have decided to limit your research to a narrowed aspect of your topic. *Use AND to narrow your search.*
- **affirmative action NOT diversity**—Use NOT to eliminate false "hits." Whether you'd want to use NOT in this case depends on the direction your research is moving. Note: In some cases, NOT is quite helpful. If you want sources that relate to written composition, search for "composition NOT music" to eliminate references to composing musical scores.

Here are some additional suggestions for developing your list of keywords:

Use "truncation" of terms to expand a search. Truncation refers to dropping letters on either side of the search term. Use right-side truncation to expand a search. For example, if you want to find information on both "astrophysics" and "astronomy" you can search for "astro" and you'll retrieve results on all words that begin with those letters.

If you don't get many results from your search, think of a list of synonyms for your topic, then insert OR between your words so that you get as expansive a list of terms as possible. For example, search for "affirmative action OR race relations OR diversity OR . . . ." As you begin getting results, you'll have a better sense of what synonyms to use.

Check the subject field of the online record for a book and/or article. You will find other subject terms listed. You can do subject searches using these terms to help you find additional references.

Examine the bibliographies of several sources. After you identify several key sources, examine the bibliographies in the back of the books. Each field uses terms differently. Thus, if you use the same keywords as are used in your sources, you'll have a better chance of finding information.

To find out how terms are used in the field of study you are exploring, read several articles on your topic and note what terms are used most frequently. Getting to know the language of your sources will help you locate appropriate information.

Write down the most important words related to your topic or to subissues about your topic.

Read at least one article or book on the topic while you are developing your keyword list. Add to your list any words you locate in that article.

4. DEVELOPING A SYSTEM FOR NOTE TAKING AND ORGANIZING SOURCES. When you begin to find valuable sources, you are ready to start taking notes. Develop a method for recording and organizing your notes, keeping track of your sources as you go.

Some researchers use a version of the popular note card technique —using one set of three-by-five-inch cards for notes and a separate set of cards for bibliographic information about the sources from which the notes are taken. Other researchers prefer keeping a research notebook in which they record the date they accessed a given item and the notes they want to have for later retrieval. Whatever your preferences, consider developing electronic equivalents, especially because of the ease with which you can download portions of texts for later use, capture lists of bibliographic data to disk, or copy and paste the location of Web sources into a separate file without making errors by retyping them. If you take time to gather snippets of information that you have downloaded, you should consider organizing that information into an electronic set of note cards. You can either put all your notes into one file, or create a separate file for each note.

5. PREPARING A WORKING BIBLIOGRAPHY.   Bibliographies are lists of books, journals, articles, recordings, Web sites, or other resources. Bibliographies sometimes cover just the literature of one academic field; other times, bibliographies cover subdisciplines or even individual authors. You can prepare a working bibliography by referring to available bibliographies on your topic or by creating your own list of sources.

Bibliographies improve the likelihood that your research will be productive. When you use a published list of resources, you are starting from a much stronger base than when you begin your search on your own; you have the results of someone else's legwork. Aided by a bibliography, you can survey a much broader list of resources in a shorter period of time.

See if your library or another library on the Internet has a specialized bibliography on your topic, a bibliography known as a reference bibliography. Sample reference bibliographies are included online in many libraries. In particular, check the Cornell Library (http://urisref.library.cornell.edu/bibliogr.htm#bibs) which includes bibliographies on the following topics, some of which were prepared for specific classes and others by faculty or librarians with an interest in the topic:

Anthropology and Archaeology	History: The Old World
Classics	The Press and Broadcasting
Contemporary Social Issues	American Government and Politics
Religion	Comparative Government
Psychology	United States Law
American Literature	Women's Studies
British Literature	Art History and Architecture
Comparative Literature	African American Studies
Philosophy	Performing Arts
Statistics	Theatre, Dance, and Film
United States History	

If you search the Web for the topic of your choice you can find bibliographies on almost any topic. Here are just a few:

Wolves: A Bibliography and Guide to the Literature

http://www.albany.edu/~knee/wolf.html

Worldwide coverage of the scientific literature about wolves for the years 1968 through 1987.

World Shakespeare Bibliography

http://www.cup.org/Shakespeare/WSBinfo.html

World Shakespeare Bibliography on CD-ROM.

Ozark Folklore: An Annotated Bibliography

http://www.system.missouri.edu/upress/otherbooks/randlore.htm

A wide range of oral traditions are included.

Mathematics Archives - Bibliographies
http://archives.math.utk.edu/bibliography.html

Includes a bibliography on chaos theory.

Bibliographies on Native Americans and the Environment
http://pantheon.cis.yale.edu/~lisamc/biblios.html

Includes information on land and water rights.

Libraries offer collections of bibliographies and post them on the Web. To explore sample bibliographies, use the Metronet collection on the World Wide Web: **http://www.metronet.lib.mn.us/lc/lc1.html**
From the home page, select US Libraries / Other Libraries / LIBCAT / Metronet. There you will find a list of topics along with the library catalog that includes a specialized bibliography on that topic. You will find that some of these databases were developed by students. Here is a portion of the listing you will find at this site:

Arizona and Southwest Index
Arizona State University
Articles in Hospitality and Tourism
Asia & Pacific Studies
Baudelaire Database
Beethoven Bibliography Database
Bible (King James Version)
Colorado Alliance of Research Lib.
Copyright Information
CORK—collection on alcoholism and substance abuse
CULT database (law)
Dartmouth College
Early American Imprints
Hazardous Waste
History of Technology Bibliography
Landmarks of Science

LASP: Current Serials about Latin America, Spain & Portugal
Librarian's Yellow Pages
Library of Congress
Maps Index
Martin Luther King Jr. Bibliography
Princeton Univ. Manuscripts Catalog
Queen's University
San Jose State University
Stanford University
Studies in Communication & Information Technology
Tilburg University
U.S. Environmental Protection Agency
University of California
Univ. of Saskatchewan— Databases
University of Surrey
Vanderbilt University

In addition to exploring the Web (and any CD-ROM databases available to you), consult print bibliographies such as the following in your library:

- *Sheehy's Guide to Reference Sources* (1986)
- *The Humanities: A Selective Guide to Information Sources* (1988)
- *Social Sciences Reference Sources: A Practical Guide* (1990)
- *The Social Sciences: A Cross-Disciplinary Guide to Selected Resources* (1989)
- *Bibliographic Index* (lists bibliographies that have been published separately or in books or journals)

6. CONTINUING YOUR SEARCH AND REEVALUATING YOUR RESEARCH PLANS.   Researching is a recursive process, a back-and-forth movement in which your topic gradually begins to emerge as you revise your list of search terms and do background reading.[1] What if your preliminary search produces limited results? In some cases, you'll find that rather than searching on a narrower topic, you need to come up with a more general search term. In other cases, you'll need to get more specific. As a rule, however, start general and then narrow your search later. You can always broaden your search again if you have to.

Planning research strategies can help get you started, but as you proceed in your research, you should be ready to switch directions and revise topics at any moment. Why? As your search continues, you will no doubt find sources that contradict some of your opinions and some of your earlier sources. As you continue searching, take time to regroup and revise your research topic as well as your research strategies. Let the new information you uncover interact with information that you found earlier in the process.

7. VALIDATING YOUR SOURCES.   All your sources need to be validated or authenticated. The Cornell Library includes a guide called "How to Critically Analyze Information Sources." Libraries have always scrutinized their acquisitions carefully, so even though it has been important to validate sources, researchers didn't have to concern themselves as much with validation of print source material as they do with Internet sources. You can also consult "Distinguishing Scholarly from Non-Scholarly Resources: A Checklist of Criteria." These sources are useful for evaluating both print and online resources.

---

[1] *The Electric Library* (http://www.elibrary.com) provides a free trial that allows new users to conduct searches for a limited time period. To get a free trial, just access the Electric Library Home Page and begin searching. You will be prompted to enter your e-mail address. In a few minutes, you will receive a password via e-mail. If you don't have access to full-text databases on your campus, you should give it a try.

Remember to evaluate your own ideas, too. Check for your own biases by asking yourself questions such as: Why do I believe this? Where did my ideas on this topic come from? Have I read any sources that challenge my original ideas?

Just because you find a source on your topic does not mean that the information is valid. In fact both print-based and Internet sources can be undependable. You must decide whether their unreliability jeopardizes the value of your research. If you are writing an opinion paper about the O.J. Simpson trial, you may not need to be concerned about the reliability of a particular opinion. Similarly, if you are doing informal research on the Civil War, it may not matter to you that the version of the Gettysburg Address is not the same as the one in the National Archives. But if you are doing a study of language use in the Gettysburg Address, you will want to know which version you are looking at. In "What Promise Does the Internet Hold for Scholars?" Raymond W. Smock explains that the Internet "contains dozens of copies of the Gettysburg Address, including a digitized image of one in Lincoln's handwriting, put on [the Internet] by the Library of Congress" (1996). Other versions put on the Internet are simple files of the text of the address, with no information about the source.

If you have gathered data from a site where university researchers are collecting information on a specialized topic, you can expect that information to be sound. If, on the other hand, you read something on a newsgroup (an online discussion group on a particular topic), you need to be more concerned about reliability. To ensure that your data is as reliable as possible, try to validate it by checking your facts in several sources—either reliable online sources or print sources. If several sources have the same information, it's more likely that the information is correct.

Some of the techniques that are useful for checking print sources can be adapted to Internet source checking. Following are some traditional ways of validating source material along with Internet variations.

1. **Check publishing company.** Is it an established press?
   Internet Applicability: Even though the Internet's e-journals (term often used for journals on the Web) are not as widely known as established presses, it is possible to find out whether the particular e-journal you are quoting is well-respected among Web scholars. Do some background research. See if the authors of the e-journal pieces have written print-based articles, too. If they have not published outside the Internet do not assume that their views are invalid. But if you do happen to learn that your source is a leading figure in the field, then you know that the Internet source is probably reliable, too.
2. **Look for footnotes.** Scholarly works almost always include citations.
   Internet Applicability: Publications on the Internet are just as likely

to have citations as their print counterparts. At times, instead of citations, the Web-based source will include a link to the "footnote" or area on the Internet where more information can be found about a given point. Be sure to check out the links.

3. **Check the date of publication.** For some topics, a study done in 1900 might be reliable; but if you are exploring public policy on a current issue, be sure that you use up-to-date information.

   Internet Applicability: Web sites typically include a "last modified" page. If you find that the page you want to quote hasn't been modified for several years, you will want to see what has been published on the topic since the Web page was created.

4. **Note whether the source validates the points you've established in other sources.**

   Internet Applicability: If you're doing a combination of library searching and Web searching, you are gradually developing a good understanding of your topic. Use your judgment. Does the Web source confirm what you've learned elsewhere? If it presents a totally different view, then you definitely need to do more investigating.

5. **See if your source material is primary or secondary.** Primary sources are direct reports from those involved (diaries, legislative bills and documents, etc.). Secondary sources are compendiums of information put together secondhand (journal articles, books, etc.).

   Internet Applicability: If you are studying the Civil War you can read histories of the period—secondary sources; if you want to read primary sources, you can find diaries and letters at the Web site for the Library of Congress.

6. **See if the presentation is impartial or biased.**

   Internet Applicability: If you are following a discussion of a topic on a mailing list, be cautious. Just because a person has strong feelings and speaks with authority does not mean that the person is correct. The author may be expressing a biased point of view, not the view that most members of a particular organization endorse. In the case of newsgroups and listserv discussion groups, you need to read many messages over several weeks before you can determine whether an individual message is typical of those submitted or whether it represents one person's bias.

7. **Check reviews.** For books, see if your source is reviewed in *Book Review Index* or *Book Review Digest*. Read several reviews and see if the reviewers agree or disagree on the value of a given book.

   Internet Applicability: There is no Internet equivalent of book reviews, although the concept of evaluating sources appears to be catching on. Yahoo (http://www.yahoo.com) and Magellan (http://mckinley.netcom.com) are two sites that have begun to place an asterisk around particularly well-designed and well-maintained sites.

8. **Note whether the author is an authority in the field.** Examine

library holdings to see what else the author has published. Notice whether the author is quoted by various sources.

Internet Applicability: Web sources often include a clickable link that returns you to the home page of the author. If possible, visit that page and see what other sources on your topic are included in the author's resume.

8. DRAFTING, REVISING, AND EDITING YOUR PAPER.   As you begin your draft, remember that a research paper should not just present the information, it should interpret it. Take time to go over your sources many times, thinking and reflecting about the issues and ideas they present. After you develop your own focus, start drafting. Present information from your perspective, being sure to use sources to support your points.

Use whatever writing process is most appropriate for you and for your topic. Some writers work best from outlines, others use jot lists, still others plunge right in and begin drafting. If you have organized your information carefully, you will be able to access your notes as you write.

During your drafting process, keep in mind that you should refocus and adjust your topic as you go. When you have questions that your current set of notes doesn't answer, return to the Web or the library and look for sources that help. Or, write to peers in your classes about issues and problems that emerge as you write.

The act of writing usually helps writers get to know their topic better than they knew it before. What you learn through research and writing may cause you to change your mind about your original thesis. Allow the drafting process to be an interactive one. Try to complete a draft so that you have a sense of direction; but as you write, continue to engage with texts and with the various information and observational research you have conducted. Keep open the possibility of doing additional research.

Revise your paper as you write, but also reserve some time toward the end of your research and writing to do a thorough revision of your text. If possible, have another reader suggest possible changes before you begin your revision session.

You will need to document your sources in your research paper. Chapter 9 focuses exclusively on citing sources. Although you don't need to worry about citation format *as* you write, you do need to make sure that you indicate the exact page reference or date in parentheses so that you will be able to locate the source later. If the author is not mentioned in your text, be sure to include the author's name in the parenthetical reference.

As you draft, revise, and edit your paper, you may want to consult various Web sites for help or additional resources. You might even want to try interactive text-based discussion areas such as MOOs or IRCs (see chapter 7) to discuss your project with others.

CONCLUSION

There is no single research process that will be right for everyone, just as there's no single writing process that works for every writer. Different writers inevitably prefer different writing and searching strategies. So customize what you do to suit your own needs, but do try to develop organized search strategies. With the array of information available on the Web, you need to be especially careful to develop sensible, yet creative research procedures.

After trying out several of the techniques suggested in this chapter, you'll be in a position to critique them and to help develop more appropriate processes for conducting library and Web research. Post your ideas to the chat area for this chapter so that readers can collaborate on a discussion of effective research and writing strategies in the information age.

END-OF-CHAPTER EXERCISES

1. Work with a group of students, either in your own class or in classes at other schools across the country to evaluate Web sources on your topic using the criteria suggested in this chapter.

2. The chapter chat section of this chapter's Web page provides you with a place to find collaborators for a bibliography for your common research needs. Consider posting problems you had in developing a shared bibliography to this forum. Or, you may be in a course where you can create your own home pages. If you develop bibliographies that you'd be willing to share with others, post a note to the forum telling the address of your home page.

SUGGESTIONS FOR RESEARCH AND WRITING

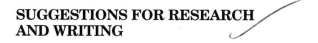

A current collection of sources related to these topics can be found at the Web site for this book.

1. Do a research project on research papers. Will the Web change the nature of the school research paper? How is it already changing it? How is it changing the college research paper? Suggestions: Examine some school-based Web sites, such as Hillside Elementary School (http://coled.umn.edu) which includes a range of hypertext research papers. Examine several college sites where students have posted Web-based research projects. Below is a list of several courses that are included on the World Lecture Hall site (http://www.utexas.edu/world/lecture). Look at these sites and others in various subject areas. Write e-mail messages to authors who invite responses and questions. Interview some writing instructors at different colleges to find out how the Web is changing the way they are presenting research assignments.

Advanced Composition

A 300-level course that uses the Internet extensively. As a final project, the class developed a Web page that includes the course syllabus, all of the course assignments, links to sites that the class members thought were valuable, and one piece of writing contributed by each student. Contains syllabus, assignments, student work, and links to related materials. By Patricia Ericsson, Dakota State University (http://www.dsu.edu/~ericssop/patty.html).

Computers and Writing

Web-based composition class. Contains syllabus, reading list, student projects, writing exercises, class roster, Internet writing resources, and message forums. By Daniel Anderson, University of Texas at Austin (http://www.en.utexas.edu/~daniel/309m).

Computers and Writing

Course focusing on the effects of digital technology and networked computers on reading, composing, communication, media, and culture. Students analyze and participate in Internet communities, write papers and compose WWW projects individually and in collaborative groups. Contains syllabus, calendar, assignments, student work, and links to related materials. By Albert Rouzie, University of Texas at Austin (http://www.crwl.utexas.edu/~Rouzie/e309sp).

2. The Internet began as a place for scientists to exchange research results. Do a project exploring either the continued nature of scientists' collaboration on the Web or the ways other researchers have begun to use the Web as a research site. For example, consider researching ways librarians are collaborating to develop new search tools and to find better ways of sharing resources. See if you can find sites on the Web where researchers post the results of their work.

CHAPTER 2

A Researcher's Introduction to the Web

Some might argue that research papers and reports have not changed all that much in spite of the Internet; yet anyone who has taken the time to learn how to use the Web for research is likely to emerge a changed writer for several reasons:

- First, using the Web skillfully can change your attitudes towards research projects. Researching a topic on the Web is lively and engaging. If you find others who are interested in the same topic, you can discover the excitement of talking through your ideas with them. When you write your paper interactively, you are more likely to have something to say than if you develop your ideas in isolation.

- Second, with the Web, you have a chance to see how your own views on a given topic compare to the views of others around the world. Even if the majority of sources you decide to cite are print-based, the experience of reading through a range of opinions on a given topic gives you a broader context for your work.

- Third, the Web allows you to find sources from more varied perspectives than you are likely to find if you limit yourself to printed books and magazines. The number and the range of materials that you can sample on the Web in a short period of time is truly amazing.

When you work on a research project, you need more than data—you often need help in understanding the topic you are researching. With the Internet, you have many ways you can pursue answers to your questions. You can send e-mail to colleagues or friends, you can post notes on discussion lists on your topic, you can join chat groups to talk with people who share your interests. You can, in effect, collaborate with other researchers no matter where they happen to live.

While the Internet has information in all disciplines and offers new ways to access that information. it is not a replacement for a library. It is, instead, a communication medium as well as a storehouse of information, just a small portion of which is the traditional kind of information you would find in a library. To learn how to use the Internet for research, you need some background information about what the Internet is and how it is organized.

WHAT IS THE INTERNET?

The Internet is a vast collection of computers that have been linked together so that many users can share their resources. The computers on the Internet are tied together in different ways: by high-speed telephone lines, by cables, and by digital networks. The computers are kept running at all times; thus, computer users from around the world can log in to them at any time of the day or night. The computers on the Internet store information and also provide users with access to e-mail and other communication tools.

The Internet was built by people from schools, colleges, and businesses across the country. It began with scientists who wanted to share research data that was confidential, top-secret information. The Internet was developed in a way that if one part of the information connection was destroyed, the other parts would still be able to connect with each other. This lack of centralization is what has inspired so many people to feel that they can play an important part in its development.

For years, the Internet was used primarily by scientists and computer programmers, since they were among the select few who knew how to transfer files from one location to another. With the advent of e-mail, however, people from all disciplines and all walks of life have become involved in the Internet. When the Gopher program (an easy-to-use way of connecting to computer sites and retrieving information) was developed at the University of Minnesota, colleges and companies around the world in all fields of study and in all areas of business began developing their own collections of information. Today, the Internet has become a truly invaluable resource for anyone willing to take the time to learn how to tap its potential.

HOW DOES THE INTERNET WORK?

Each computer on the Internet sends data to and receives data from other computers in small bundles of computer code called packets. When you transmit a message or other information, the packets of computer data are sent through many paths over the millions of networks that constitute the Internet. The individual packets don't always travel the same route. But no matter how they reach their destination, they are automatically reassembled at the end of the path.

You can access the Internet in two ways: by modem or by direct access. If you are a student, you probably have direct access to the Internet from a campus computer lab; but you may need to purchase a modem (mo[dulator]+dem[odulator]) to connect to the Internet from your residence hall or home. If you work for a company that has direct Internet connectivity on site, you may also need to be able to access your account through a modem from home.

MODEM ACCESS.   Using special software with your computer and a modem, you can "call" a computer that is directly on the Internet. You need an account on that computer—a login name (a name which the computer knows you by), a password, software for connecting with the Internet through your service provider, and a storage area where your e-mail can be deposited. You should use the fastest modem you can afford. Modem speeds are measured in bauds per second (bps). You need at least a 14.4 bps, preferably a 28.8 bps, modem. The information you are moving back and forth through your modem between distant computers and your computer should move at the fastest speed possible so that you don't have lots of delays.

With a modem, you can have what is known as either a shell connection or a PPP (point-to-point protocol) connection to the Internet. With a shell connection, your computer functions as a keyboard or input device for a computer at your school or company. You use the computing power of the remote computer instead of the power of your own computer to connect to Internet sites. In most cases, you cannot view graphics with this kind of account. With a PPP connection, your computer is temporarily on the Internet, even though it establishes its connection by using a phone line to connect to a direct Internet connection at another site. With a PPP connection, you use the computing power of your own computer while you are on the Internet. You can use a program such as Netscape or Microsoft Explorer and save Internet files directly to your own disks, or you can attach formatted files to an e-mail program such as Eudora and send them to your classmates.

Companies such as America Online and Prodigy offer a communication package that connects you to their services and also provides you with a gateway (or way of accessing) the Internet and the World Wide Web. These companies charge a monthly fee for their services with the hope that you will access the Internet through them. In addition to providing you with access to the Web, they provide resources such as encyclopedias, software, and other supplementary offerings to entice you to use their services.

DIRECT ACCESS.   With a direct connection, you can access the Internet at much faster speeds than with dial-up modem access. If you do not have direct access from home, you should take advantage of the speed of connections at school or office and do much of your searching from there. In particular, if you want to display and view Web documents that have graphics, you will need fast Internet access. Many colleges and businesses have recently upgraded their networks to provide sufficient bandwidth (the amount of information that can pass through the cable at a time) for graphics and even short movies to be displayed.

WHAT IS THE CONNECTION BETWEEN THE WORLD WIDE WEB AND THE INTERNET?

The World Wide Web is that portion of the Internet that has been developed in hypertext—or linked—format, allowing you to move from one Web location to another by clicking on highlighted links. Until a few years ago, Web sites constituted only a small share of the information resources on the Internet. Today, the Web is the largest part of the Internet. (Other Internet areas such as Gopher sites, FTP sites, and Telnet sites described later in this chapter are now accessible through Web software.)

Being connected to the Web means being connected to the interconnected set of networks that constitute the Internet. Each of the individual networks on the Internet is maintained by the owners—individuals, school or college representatives, or Web creators in other organizations. Some Internet networks are faster and more high-powered than others. NSFNET, maintained by the National Science Foundation, links supercomputers across the country and allows information from less powerful networks to travel long routes on its network. Companies called service providers own and maintain many of the large and small Internet communication lines.

WHAT IS ON THE WEB?

Until a few years ago the Internet was primarily used by scientists and computer scientists; thus, there was only minimal information about the humanities or social sciences available on the Web. In the last few years, however, museums, libraries, businesses, government agencies, and universities have established impressive Web sites and Gopher sites. Researchers in all disciplines are now using the Internet to share information and to discuss their fields.

The information resources that have been collected on the Internet consist of a wide variety of material—digitized versions of traditional library information along with totally new sources of information, ranging from previously hard-to-find texts to totally new collections of images that have been developed exclusively because of and for the Internet. For example, you can view art history collections on the Art History Server (http://www.137.141.153.38/art.html). Or you can explore the World Wide Web Anthropology Library (http://Elab-server.usc.edu/ANTHROPOLOGY.HTML). You can even access photographs from a collection at the Smithsonian (FTP://photo1.sci.edu).

WHAT DO YOU NEED TO KNOW ABOUT THE WEB?

You need to know how to navigate and how to find information on the Web, and you'll learn how to do that in chapter 3. But first, you should understand some basic concepts. Here are some questions and answers about some essential features of the Internet and the World Wide Web:

1. What is a home page?   The term *home page* is used to refer to the first "page" or screen in a given set of pages or screens that function as starting points for Web viewing. The home page often functions as an index of sorts—a guide to the other resources available at either the current site or other locations. For example, most colleges now have home pages with pointers to other places on campus, such as the library. The library page, in turn provides information and also lists resources on other libraries' home pages in different parts of the world. Each home page has its own Internet address which describes the exact location of the computer and the file. Figure 2.1 shows the home page for the Library of Congress. Note that the hypertext links point users to other services offered by the library, such as "General Information and Publications" and "Research and Collections Services."

This book has its own home page (http://www.prenhall.com/rodrigues) which contains information to supplement the chapters in this book plus interactive forums where readers can interact with one another. If you haven't already, check out this page and visit it regularly.

If you want to add information to the Web, you need to develop a home page or place information on someone else's home page. You can store the page on your own computer or disk for private use. If you store your home page on a computer that has been set up as a Web site, you can share your research results with others.

2. What is a browser?   A browser is a software program (such as Lynx,

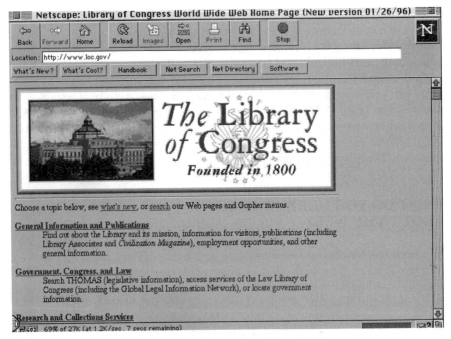

Figure 2.1   Library of Congress Home Page as viewed through Netscape.

Netscape, or Microsoft Explorer) that lets you view the contents of the Web. It is designed to enable you to jump easily from one Web location to another. Sometimes browsers also provide access to non-Web information resources on the Internet such as collections of information on Gopher servers and computer databases around the world.

How the Web is displayed to you depends on whether you are using a graphical or a text-based browser. Graphical browsers such as Netscape show both the formatted text and the images; the hypertext links are underlined. Text browsers such as Lynx display only plain text, not graphics. The hypertext links are displayed as either numbers or highlights on the page. Figure 2.1 shows the Library of Congress Home Page as viewed through Netscape, the most widely used graphical browser.

With Lynx, shown in Figure 2.2, the same page would look quite different, though the text-based information is identical.

How can the same page look so different with different browsers? The developers of the Web, researchers at CERN (European Laboratory for Particle Physics) in Switzerland, created a method that would enable Web pages to be viewed on both high-end platforms and low-end machines. They developed Hypertext Markup Language (HTML), a system for marking up pages with code to indicate how each page should be viewed on the

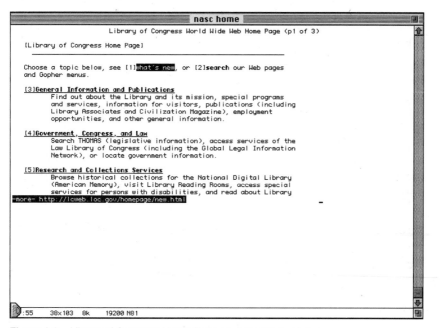

Figure 2.2   Library of Congress Home Page as viewed through Lynx.

computer screen. The source code is the same for each page. Source code, the text that has been "marked up" with commands such as <TITLE> and <CENTER>, tells your browser how to display the page on your screen. The code is hidden from your view, but you can see it in Netscape by clicking on **View** and then selecting **Document Source** or in Lynx by pressing the backslash key <\> . The same code, when translated by browsers Lynx and Netscape, is displayed in dramatically different ways. Figure 2.3 shows a portion of the Library of Congress Home Page as it looks when viewed as source code.

Browsers filter text much as some kinds of glass lenses filter light. Just as dark glasses make the world look different from the way it looks through clear lenses, so a graphical browser allows HTML code to take on different characteristics than does a text-based filter.

3. How is a site named?   You may have noticed the unusual way of addressing sites in the examples in this chapter (http://www.something.com), and you may be wondering how this convention emerged. Site names on the Internet follow elaborate schemes that provide information to computers. All computers have an organization name and a domain suffix that indicates what type of organization is hosting the computer for a

```
<html>

<HEAD>
<TITLE>Library of Congress World Wide Web Home
Page</TITLE>
<base href="http://lcweb.loc.gov/homepage/lchp.html">
</HEAD>

<BODY>

<center><IMG SRC="http://lcweb.loc.gov/homepage/lchp_v1.gif"
ALT="[Library of Congress Home Page]"></center>
<HR>
Choose a topic below, see <a
href="http://lcweb.loc.gov/homepage/new.html">what's
new</a>, or <a
href="http://lcweb.loc.gov/harvest/">search</a> our Web pages
and Gopher menus.
<p>
<DL>
<DT><STRONG><a
href="http://lcweb.loc.gov/homepage/genpub.html">General
Information and Publications</a></STRONG>
<DD>Find out about the Library and its mission, special
programs and services, information for visitors, publications
(including Library Associates and <cite>Civilization
Magazine</cite>), employment opportunities, and other general
information.
<P>
<DT><STRONG><A
HREF="http://lcweb.loc.gov/homepage/govt.html">Government,
Congress, and Law</A></STRONG>
<DD>Search THOMAS (legislative information), access services
of the Law Library of Congress (including the Global Legal
Information Network), or locate government information.
 <P>
<DT><STRONG><A
HREF="http://lcweb.loc.gov/homepage/rschcoll.html">Research
and Collections Services</A></STRONG>
<DD>Browse historical collections for the National Digital
Library (American Memory), visit Library Reading Rooms,
access special services for persons with disabilities, and read
about Library of Congress cataloging, acquisitions, and
preservation operations and policy.
<P>
```

Figure 2.3   Source code for Lynx and Netscape.

particular account. The following box lists common domain suffixes and the type of organization each represents:

Domain Suffix	*Organization Type*
.com	Commercial organization
.edu	Educational
.org	Non-commercial organization
.mil	Military
.gov	Government

Addressing schemes are important to understand, too. Each site on the Internet has a Uniform Resource Locator or URL. This addressing scheme is done uniformly across the world, and entering it correctly makes it possible for you to "locate" the site and the specific information at that site that you want. The URL is the address for the computer data itself. Each URL has three parts:

Type of Web Access	*Name of Computer/ Organization*	*Domain Suffix*
http	www.prenhall	.com
http	ajax.prenhall	.com

Most Internet sites today are Web sites and thus begin with **http,** an acronym for Hypertext Transfer Protocol. But some URLs begin with **gopher;** others begin with **ftp,** some begin with **news,** and still others begin with **telnet.** The following box explains these address terms:

HTML, Gopher, FTP, and Telnet

HTML

Html sites (**Hypertext Markup Language**) are sites that are part of the World Wide Web. Web sites that have been marked up using Hypertext Markup Language are addressed with http://

Example: **http://www.infoseek.com**

This is the address for Infoseek, a search tool you'll learn about in chapter 3.

Gopher

Gopher sites store information using the hierarchical menu-based software known as Gopher.

Example: **gopher://gopher.macfdn.org:3016**

This is a database of information about the John D. and Catherine T. MacArthur Foundation.

FTP

FTP or File Transfer Protocol sites allow you to transfer files from another computer to your own.

Example: **ftp://ifcss.org**

This address takes you to a set of news releases from the Academic Exchange Information Center.

Telnet

Telnet sites are accessed through a program called Telnet. Telnet stands for telephone network. When you type a Telnet address into your browser or when you click on a Telnet address, you are really launching a Telnet session. (Note: At the time of this writing, Telnet is still an add-on program that must be resident on your computer for Netscape or another browser to respond to the Telnet addressing scheme.)

Example: **telnet://cuinfo2.cit.cornell.edu**

This is the Telnet address for the Cornell University Library.

4. How are different kinds of Internet sites accessed?   Until recently, researchers who wanted to find information on the Internet had to use separate programs to find different kinds of Internet sites, including Gopher sites, FTP sites, and Telnet sites. For example, you would have had to use special Gopher software to reach Gopher sites. To access FTP sites you would have needed to know how to launch an FTP session. To log in to computers at other sites, you would have had to know how to use Telnet. Unless you want to learn how to do more sophisticated research, you no longer need to know how to use separate programs, since they have been incorporated into most World Wide Web browsers (software programs that enable you to navigate the Web) such as Netscape and Microsoft Explorer.

PRACTICE BOX

1. Learn how to access the Web. Try to access the sites described in this chapter. (Realize that they may no longer look exactly like they do here. Nor will the links necessarily be the same.) If you have Web access in your library, ask a librarian for help if you need it. Jot down any answers you get and share them with your classmates.

2. Learn as much as you can about Web access from your campus or place of employment. Find out what restrictions there are on your account. Find out if your browser has e-mail integrated into it. Find out if you have PPP access from off-campus sites.

---

5. How are Internet sites developed?   The Web is a democratic place. The information that has been put on the Web has been collected by all kinds of people, including students in college classes. Everyone has an equal opportunity to contribute to its continually expanding information resources. An Internet collection of research on knot theory developed by a group of students at Claremont High School in California (http://www. cusd.claremont.edu) is in many ways just as important and as useful to a researcher who needs the available information as a site developed by research scientists at NASA.

Many Web sites are set up to encourage people to contribute data to them. One such place is the Internet Public Library (http://ipl.sils. umich.edu/), whose home page includes this suggestion:

> If you'd like to suggest a resource to be added to this collection, please fill out our Recommendation Form or send e-mail to ipl.ref.url@umich.edu.

You might want to develop your own Web collection. If you want to collaborate in developing a database of information with others in your class or place of employment, we hope you'll link your information to the Web site for this text. Contributions made to the Web site for this book can be a starting point for a collection on using the Web for research papers.

In spite of its largely democratic nature, a growing number of Web sites are not open to the public. To access resources such as the *Encyclopaedia Britannica* and many CD-ROM databases, you need to have an account with a school or business that pays for a subscription. Many Internet enthusiasts feel strongly that information resources should be made available to everyone freely. To make the Internet a viable option for students and citizens across the country, people are volunteering to help develop information sources. For example, an encyclopedia called *The Free Encyclopedia* is being developed by librarians Clif Davis and Margaret Adamson Fincannon (http://clever.net/cam/encyclopedia.html). The only problem with sources on the "free Internet" is that the entries tend not to be checked for validity as rigorously as similar copyrighted sources.

If you haven't yet explored the Internet, you may be surprised to discover that many sites you visit are "under construction," that is, just rough drafts of what the developers hope their home page and accompanying pages will become. In actuality, all sites are under continual construction and reconstruction. What you see one day of the week may be different the next day. Unlike a printed resource that has to go through a long process before publication, Web sites can be published swiftly and disappear just as swiftly. Nonetheless, they are ideal environments for continual revision because changes can be made quickly.

CONCLUSION

The Internet is rapidly increasing in size. In 1993, there were several hundred sites on the Web. At the writing of this book, there are more than 15,000 Web servers and millions of documents. Clearly, the Web is a convenient way of sharing information and keeping it up-to-date. There are other reasons for the continual expansion of the Web: business, industry, and schools can save on mailings by providing information online; they can also improve their image by providing carefully designed and information-rich pages. And libraries can make collections available to everyone. The spirit of reciprocity that has emerged stimulates people to want to share with others. People have found that if they provide information, others will return the favor.

Is the Web essential for research? Bruce Dobler and Harry Bloomberg think so. Writing in a chapter of a recent book, they say that Web research should be part of standard research processes:

> It isn't a matter anymore of using computer searches to locate existing documents buried in some far-off library or archive. The Web is providing documents and resources that simply would be too expensive to publish on paper or CD-ROM.
> Right now—and not in some distant future—doing research without looking for resources on the Internet is, in most cases, not really looking hard enough. . . . A thorough researcher cannot totally avoid the Internet and the Web. (Galen & Latchaw 1997)

If you visit the Web site for this book frequently, you will have a chance to contribute information to the Web and to enjoy the added value the Web offers—the opportunity to collaborate with others with similar interests. The Web is more than a set of information resources; it is a way of connecting people.

END-OF-CHAPTER EXERCISES

1. Examine the web sites referred to in this chapter. Which is the best organized? Most effective? Least effective? Why?
2. Visit the Web site for this chapter and complete the online exercises. Contribute to the Web Chat forum, a place for you to respond to questions proposed by the author or by other students and to discuss your answers.

SUGGESTIONS FOR RESEARCH AND WRITING

A current collection of sources related to these topics can be found at the Web site for this book.

Below are some general Web-related writing topics. If you begin searching for information now, you can continue gathering data as you read other chapters in this text. Your research project may not be Web-intensive; nonetheless, consider beginning early and working on your topic as you progress through the chapters of this book. Take time to find a topic that interests you, whether you have prescribed assignments or not. Here are some ideas you can consider writing about:

1. Have you been following the rapid development of the World Wide Web? Would you like to learn more about what is happening? Write a report on effective or ineffective uses of the Web in different settings. Explore uses of the Web on different campuses or businesses as well as on your own campus or in your own place of employment. Take a stand on some aspect of Web use or Web policy. Document your position by referring to specific information (examples of home pages of other schools, interviews you conduct via e-mail, etc.).

Here are some questions you might explore:

- Are campuses and/or businesses sufficiently responsive to student or employee needs? faculty needs? community needs?
- Are computer centers supporting the needs of faculty and students?
- Are faculty and students building their own computer environments when there is no response from the computer center or the administration?
- Why is your campus computing or business computing environment better/worse than other places?

Here are some issues to consider:

- Should all students be required to purchase a computer when they enroll in college?
- Should computers be provided and the purchase price be built into the tuition price? (Note: In most schools, students are from varying financial backgrounds and not all can afford personal computers. In spite of this disparity, professors do most class communication through the Web.)

2. If you no longer watch much television but do devote considerable time to computers, you may be interested in this topic possibility: Explore the potential for the Web and television to merge into one medium. What are the implications for schools? for training programs for business and industry? What is happening in this area already? What kinds of television courses would be best for home-schooled children? for adults exploring second careers?

3. If you are interested in freedom of information issues, this topic may be one you'll want to explore: Do you think that the Internet and the World Wide Web will democratize countries that have not had open access to information? Is the Internet giving more power to formerly disenfranchised groups in the United States? Explore information access in different countries, with particular emphasis on the Internet and the Web. As you get a sense of what is happening, take a stand and support your point with data that you collect from your sources.

4. Do you believe in Web censorship? Explore the issues related to Web censorship and take a stand. Issues to consider: pornography and children; surf-patrol programs in the schools; freedom of information acts.

5. Have you thought about what effect the Internet and the Web will have in your home community? What about on the concept of community in general? Some have argued that new Internet communities are developing (*The Virtual Community: Homesteading on the Electronic Frontier,* Rheingold, 1993) that replace the old back-porch communities in small towns. Is this phenomenon accurate? Is it a positive or negative development? Take a stand, but substantiate your opinion with ample data.

CHAPTER 3

THE BASICS OF WEB NAVIGATION

For more than a decade, technology has been making a dramatic impact on libraries. Electronic library catalogs have replaced card catalogs. CD-ROM databases have been made widely available both in libraries and (for subscribers) on the Web. In addition, many college and university libraries now offer their students and staff online access to a range of bibliographic databases that include the full texts of thousands of periodical articles. Today, researchers suffer from an embarrassment of riches: they have so many sources available to them that they need to be extremely critical as they select the best information for their research projects.

By learning how to access and use the World Wide Web to conduct research, you will be able to search many libraries across the globe; you also will be able to search computer archives on specialized topics and survey or interview experts who can provide the kind of immediacy to your research that traditional resources can't begin to approximate.

By familiarizing yourself with the kinds of information available through the Web, you will enlarge the scope of your research projects while developing information literacy useful for lifelong needs. Not only will you be able to find books and text-based resources, but also you will be able to find medical information, check on your investments, and make travel plans. Before you can conduct sophisticated research, however, you need to master the basics. In this chapter you will learn the basics of Internet access. For a discussion of more advanced searching techniques, see chapter 6, "Researching the Disciplines."

NAVIGATION TECHNIQUES

There are many ways to locate information and move around or "navigate" the World Wide Web. This chapter will cover four basic ways to explore the Web: using the navigation panel along with the home page; using search tools; typing in Uniform Resource Locators; and using bookmarks as placeholders for future navigation.

The Navigation Panel and the Home Page

The term *home page* refers to the opening page or index for a given Web site as well as to the first page that loads when you launch your Web browser. Other pages that you visit within a given site are simply referred to as pages. From the start-up home page, you can move to many locations, depending on the hypertext links that have been incorporated into the page you are using. Sometimes links are underlined text areas; other times, such as on Prentice Hall's home page, they are "buttons" (boxed areas) that allow you to jump to additional information about each item. From the home page for Prentice Hall (see figure 3.1) you can jump to information about any of the subject areas included in boxes. After you go to one area, you can jump to other clickable areas listed on each succeeding page you visit. You can use the navigation panel (control panel with buttons) on your browser to move **Back** to each previous location you have visited. If you click on **Home,** you will return to the start-up page. You use the buttons and other items on the navigation panel in conjunction with the hypertext links to move from page to page.

Learn how to do the following: use the hypertext links to jump to either another Web page or to a totally new site; move to a previous page (using the **Back** button); move forward a page at a time using the **Forward** button; and use the **Go** feature to see all the sites you've explored and to revisit a previous site (sometimes called **History**). Locate these buttons in Prentice Hall's home page in figure 3.1.

If you would like to change your browser's start-up or home page, you can. Why would you want to do this? You may find a home page somewhere on the Web that suits your needs more than the one that you have. If you are a physics major, for example, you may want to set your home page to The Internet Pilot to Physics (http://www.tp.umu.se/TIPTOP/about.html). If you are an English major, you might choose to have the On-Line Books Page (http://www.cs.cmu.edu/Web/books.html) as your home page. History majors might set their home page to WWW U.S. History Resources (http://www.arts.gla.ac.uk/www/ctich/histlinks.html).

With Netscape, you change your home page in this way: Click and hold down **Option** on the menu bar then select **General Preferences.** In the middle of the screen you should see the following:

```
Browser starts with :
o Blank Page
o Home Page Location: http://YOURLOCATION.edu:70/0/home
```

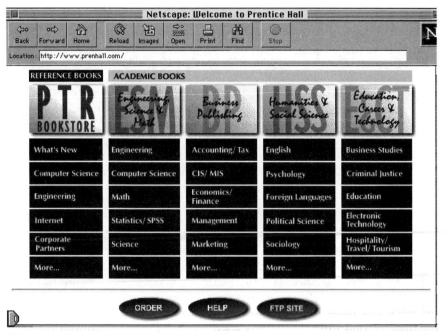

Figure 3.1   Prentice Hall's home page.

To change your home page location, erase the existing address and type in the address of your choice. You can change your home page with Lynx, too. First save the page of your preferred site. Use a descriptive name so you'll remember it. (Type **h** from the Lynx program to access the help menu and learn how to save pages.) Then, instead of typing **lynx** to launch Lynx, you type **lynx descriptive_name.** For example, if you want to use a location such as the Library of Congress as your home page, you would save the Library of Congress Home Page as something like libcong.html. Then you could launch this page with Lynx by typing lynx libcong.html.

Navigation with a graphical browser is much different from navigation with a text-based browser. With a graphical browser such as Netscape, you point and click with the mouse to jump from hyperlink to hyperlink. With most versions of Lynx, you do not connect directly to the Web through your own computer; rather, your computer must connect to the World Wide Web through a computer that runs the UNIX operating system. UNIX is not a point-and-click environment. You move around the Web using either letter commands or arrow keys. For example, some basics for navigating the Internet with Lynx include: using the right arrow to go to a new site, using the left arrow to move to a previous site, using the up and down arrows to move either to the top or bottom of a page, and using the tab key to move from one highlighted or underlined link to the next.

PRACTICE BOX

1. List the steps you take to access the World Wide Web.
2. Experiment with home page selection. Find a home page that seems more suitable to your needs than your current home page and change the preferences in your browser.
3. Discuss problems that you have in navigating the Web with your browser. Help one another solve these problems.

Search Tools

Computer programs that help you retrieve information from databases are called search tools. You are familiar with the kinds of search tools that are used in library catalogs. These tools typically allow you to search by subject, author, or title. Since librarians use a standard set of key words from the Library of Congress Subject Headings, library searching is easier to conduct than Web searching. (See chapter 5 for a discussion of library searching.)

Unlike a library, the Internet has no common set of subject headings or categories. Everyone who contributes information to the Internet organizes information arbitrarily and uses different terms. Fortunately, search engines—computer programs that index information on the Internet— have been developed to assist you in your Internet search. Computers can search through millions of files and report results to you in seconds.

There are two basic ways of accessing Web information: (1) search engines that search entire Web databases and (2) subject directories—categorized lists of information—often with search engines available to search the individual lists or the entire Web.

To locate a collection of search tools in Netscape, press the **Net Search** button on the menu bar and move toward the end of the page to view the list of search tools listed (see figure 3.2). To access a catalog of information in Lynx, type **i** to access the meta-index (see figure 3.3). After you have used a few search tools, you will want to "bookmark" your favorites for easier access (bookmarks are explained later in this chapter).

Search Engines.   Search engines use a robot computer program to scour the Web for sites and return results to a main database. Search engines work in different ways. The relative strength or weakness of a search engine depends on how "good the search engine is at locating what you need and presenting it in a usable way," according to Roy Tennant (*Syllabus,* February 1996, 36–38). The automated breed of search systems, including WebCrawler, Infoseek, Lycos, Open Text, and Alta Vista, use

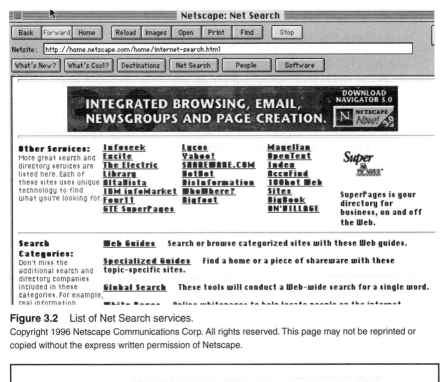

Figure 3.2   List of Net Search services.

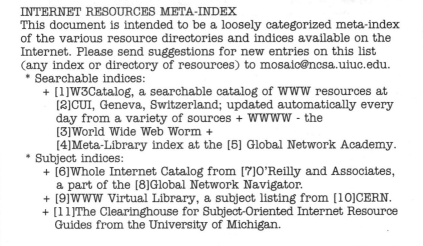

INTERNET RESOURCES META-INDEX
This document is intended to be a loosely categorized meta-index of the various resource directories and indices available on the Internet. Please send suggestions for new entries on this list (any index or directory of resources) to mosaic@ncsa.uiuc.edu.
* Searchable indices:
    + [1]W3Catalog, a searchable catalog of WWW resources at [2]CUI, Geneva, Switzerland; updated automatically every day from a variety of sources + WWWW - the [3]World Wide Web Worm + [4]Meta-Library index at the [5] Global Network Academy.
* Subject indices:
    + [6]Whole Internet Catalog from [7]O'Reilly and Associates, a part of the [8]Global Network Navigator.
    + [9]WWW Virtual Library, a subject listing from [10]CERN.
    + [11]The Clearinghouse for Subject-Oriented Internet Resource Guides from the University of Michigan.

Figure 3.3   Internet Resources meta-index.

computer programs that rove the Internet continually to gather information about new sites and to report that information to the search engine's computer. New search engines are being created all the time.

WebCrawler
http://www.webcrawler.com

WebCrawler is perhaps the speediest search tool on the Internet. It indexes documents on the Web and returns results in simple list fashion. At least 2,000 new sites are added each month. WebCrawler was purchased by America Online in 1995. In the spirit of sharing that has become characteristic of Web culture, America Online provides open access to WebCrawler, even to people who are on the Web and not subscribers.

WebCrawler does what is called proximity searching (see figure 3.4). That is, it assumes that the terms you enter should be found on the same page. If you search for information about affirmative action, you would certainly want the terms to be found on the same page, not just anywhere in the document.

WebCrawler is especially useful if you know the specific name of a company or Web site that you want to locate since the default (built-in) setting returns only a list of "hits." The advantage of seeing only a list is that you can quickly scan the list to see what it contains. The disadvantage

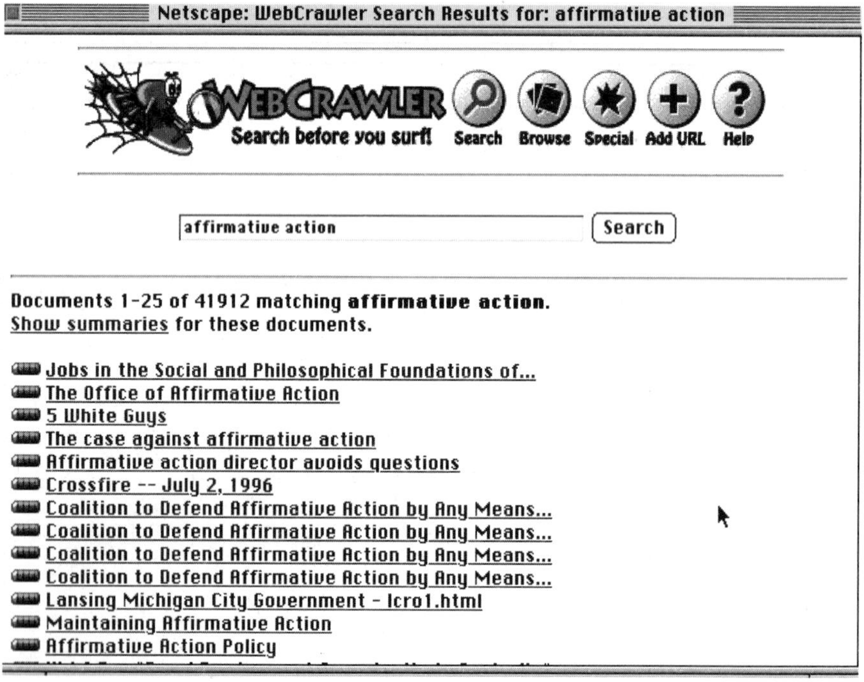

Figure 3.4   Search results in WebCrawler.

is that you can't tell what kind of information is on the page. If you want a summary of the site, you can check "show summaries" on the WebCrawler home page.

Infoseek

http://www2.infoseek.com

Infoseek is one of the most comprehensive search tools on the Web. Currently its database contains more than 400,000 documents. The results of your search include a computer-generated abstract of the information available at the sites your search has identified. The computer selects phrases on each page at random to provide a sense of the information available. This feature enables you to tell whether a particular site is appropriate for your needs.

For example, in the sample page in figure 3.5, Mike's Conservative Home Page is clearly an individual person's home page that expresses that person's opinion. You would probably not want to use a source unless you made it clear to your reader that the information is merely one person's opinion.

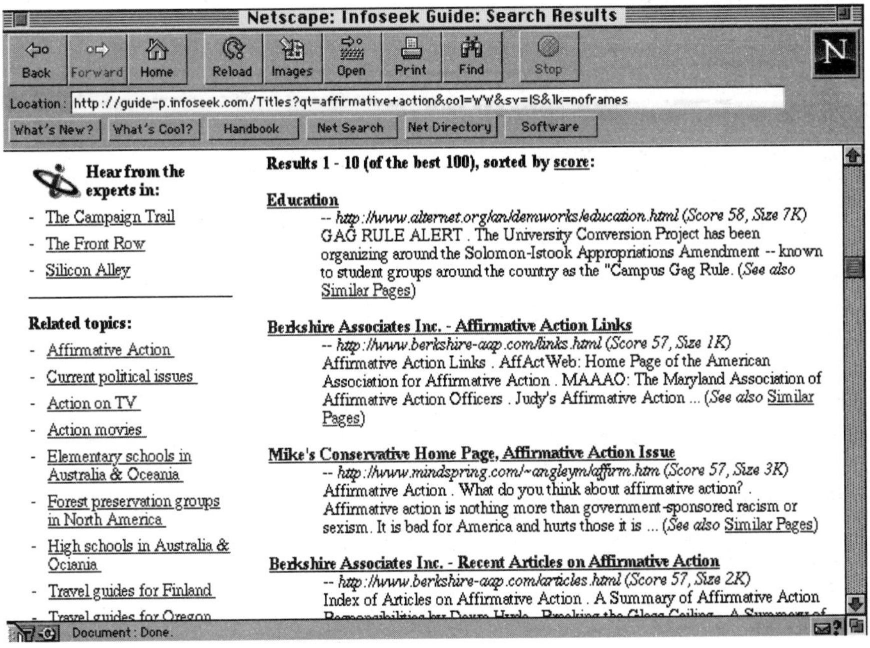

Figure 3.5   Search results in Infoseek.

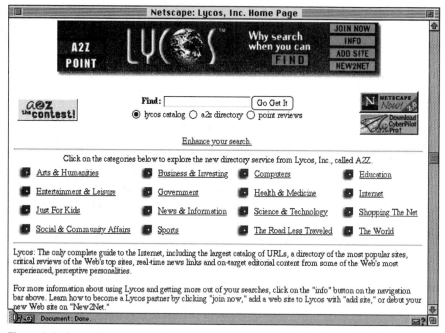

Figure 3.6   Lycos Home Page.

Lycos

http://www.lycos.com/

Instead of just returning a list of sites by name, Lycos returns a machine-generated abstract of the information so that you can decide whether or not to visit the site. The Lycos index is built by a robot program that visits every link on every site on the Internet. The Lycos catalog currently holds nearly eight million documents—more than 90 percent of the documents on the Internet. A subject directory called Lycos 250 is scheduled to be added to the Lycos Home Page. The Lycos Home Page as of this writing is shown in figure 3.6. Lycos allows users to set options, such as whether their search term is a word or a phrase or whether they want to exclude certain words from their search using Boolean operators (see chapter 1).

Open Text

http://www.opentext.com:8080/

Open Text indexes more than one million documents on the Web. The Its databases index every word on every page. Not only is this service fast,

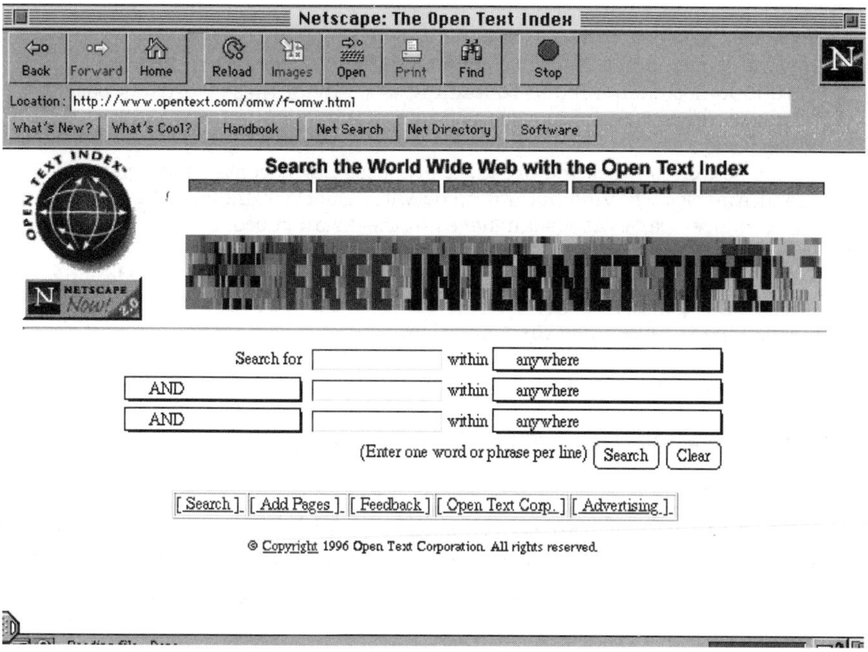

Figure 3.7 Open Text home page.

but also it provides you with several ways to control your search. You can select Simple Search, Power Search, or Weighted Search. Simple Search does a phrase search by default. (In a phrase search, the computer looks for documents that use the terms you enter—e.g., affirmative action—as a unit.) Power Search allows users to use Boolean operators (see chapter 1). Weighted Search gives you a chance to indicate with numbers the relative importance of the search terms you use. The Open Text home page is shown in figure 3.7.

Alta Vista

http://www.digital.altavista.com/

Alta Vista uses what is called associative searching. That is, if you search for any keyword, you receive a list of related topics that you can explore. Alta Vista's help screen explains how this works:

. . . suppose you wanted information about the languages of American Indians and you did the following query: american indian language, here's what you would observe.

american indian language
result:
   word count: indian 395185, language 2048030, american 2654433.
   100000 documents found containing as many of these words as possible,
   in both upper and lower case.
observation:
   This search is much too broad. It produces pages containing american
   and American having nothing to do with American Indians. In addition,
   it produces pages about languages in the Asian subcontinent.
strategy:
   Make clear how you want the query to be parsed. In other words, link
   american and indian together as a phrase. Also, so that the plural of
   language is found, use the * notation.

"american indian" language*
result:
   word count: american indian 30000, language* 2050463. 20000
   documents

Use the results of your search skillfully. Add the keywords it suggests
to your growing list of words and do a few additional searches using those
keywords. The home page for Alta Vista is shown in figure 3.8.

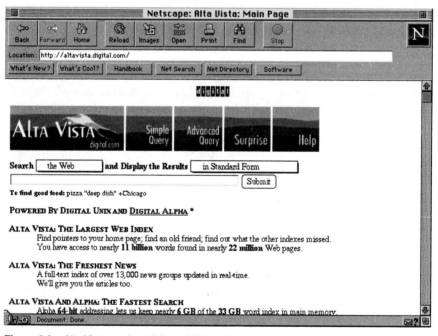

Figure 3.8   Alta Vista as viewed through Netscape.

Categorized Lists.   Subject directories such as Yahoo and the World Wide Web Virtual Library are created by people, not merely by programs that scour the Web looking for sites that match a search request. Results are more focused, and often more useful to a researcher, than are the results obtained by using search engines alone. Subject directories use broad subject categories and more specific sub-categories to help users browse for the most appropriate category for their needs. For a discussion of subject directories particularly useful for different disciplines, see chapter 6.

PRACTICE BOX

1. Use the chart below to record your exploration of different search engines. Search for the topics suggested or provide your own topics. See which of the search tools generates the best results.

Number of useful hits on terms listed below:	Web- Crawler	Info- seek	Lycos	Alta Vista	Open Text
Affirmative action					
Technology and higher education					
Add your topic here:					
Add your topic here:					

2. As you use different search engines, experiment with both simple searching and advanced searching. Notice how different search engines conduct their searches. Take notes on some key differences and share your insights with your classmates.

Yahoo

http://www.yahoo.com/

Yahoo is one of the most respected subject directories on the Internet. Yahoo began modestly: two Stanford University students created it as a way to keep track of resources related to their personal interests. Many of the resources include brief summaries. The largest hierarchical index on the Web, Yahoo's home page includes dozens of categories and a search engine that lets you search all of Yahoo, just the category you are

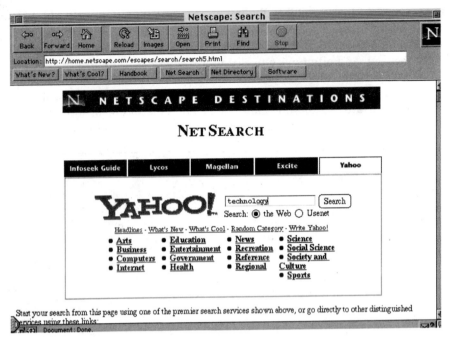

Figure 3.9   Yahoo as viewed through Netscape.

examining, or the entire Web. Clicking on each category brings up many narrower lists of items. When you select an item, you "jump" to that site. Yahoo should be one of the first places on the Web that you browse for information on any topic. Try scrolling through the many categories on the list before searching. Figure 3.9 shows the home page for Yahoo.

The World Wide Web Virtual Library

http://www.w3.org/hypertext/DataSources/bySubject/Overview.html/

The World Wide Web Virtual Library is a distributed system. That is, its various categories are maintained by people with expertise on the topic who work on their computers at institutions throughout the world rather than on a computer at one location. An advantage to searching a distributed system is that the various categories are maintained by subject experts, not generalists; a disadvantage is that users cannot search the entire contents of its collection, since its collection does not reside in one place. The home page for the World Wide Web Virtual Library is shown in figure 3.10.

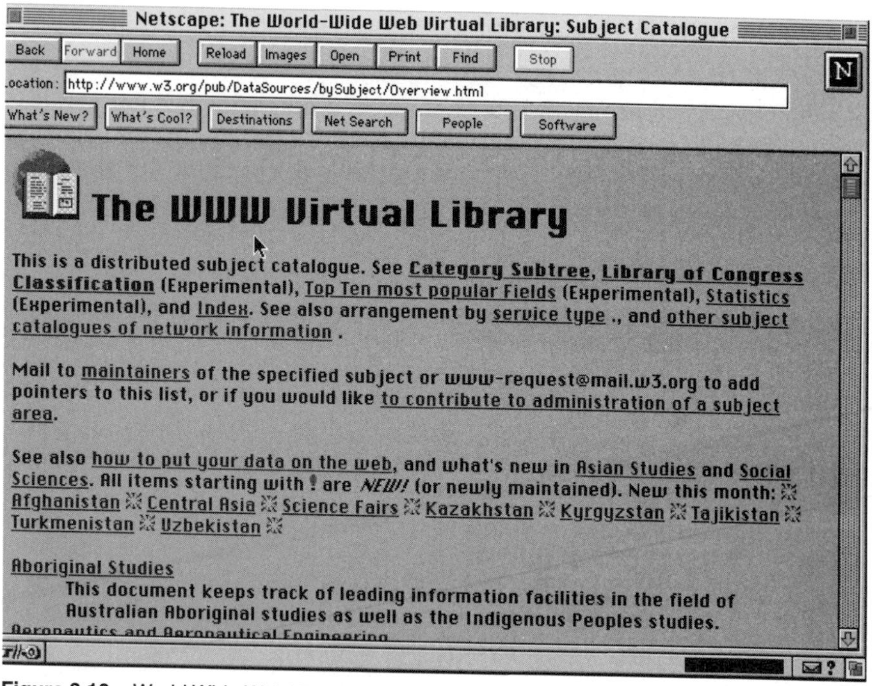

Figure 3.10   World Wide Web Virtual Library page.

PRACTICE BOX

1. Select two search tools and explore your topic. Compare the results of your search, not only in terms of the number of hits but in terms of the value of the information you locate. Change your search terms and repeat the search. Discuss the value of searching several times with slightly different combinations of keywords.

2. Search for your topic in a categorized subject site. First, search at the top level for a topic such as affirmative action. Then navigate down to a subcategory such as education and search again. What is the advantage of narrowing a category before searching?

3. Do a library search on a topic of your choice using the online catalog in your library. Compare the results of your library search and your Web search. Does the Web provide alternative insights into your topic?

The Uniform Resource Locator (URL)

You may read about an Internet site in a magazine or hear about it on television. How do you get to that site easily? The address for each site on the Internet is called the URL Uniform Resource Locator. To access that site, you type the address into the appropriate area of your browser. In Netscape, you select **File** then click on **Open URL** and enter the address. For example, the URL for Netscape Corporation is

http://www.netscape.com

Not all URLs are addresses for Web sites. URLs can also point to Gopher sites, File Transfer Protocol (FTP) sites, newsgroups, or Telnet sites. The address for this book is a Web address:

http://prenhall.com/rodrigues

Some sites have different addresses for different services. For example, the Clearinghouse for Subject-Oriented Internet Resource Guides can be accessed in the following ways:

Web: **http://www.lib.umich.edu/chhome.html**

Gopher: **gopher://gopher.lib.umich.edu**

FTP: **ftp://una.hh.lib.umich.edu**

Be careful when you enter the addresses into your computer. Most information on the Internet is not case-sensitive (that is, requiring upper- or lowercase letters), but some portions of WWW addresses are. Internet e-mail addresses can be written in either upper- or lowercase and they'll still arrive at their destination. You can write to the author of this book at either drodrigues@utb1.utb.edu or Drodrigues@UTB1.UTB.edu.

But the filenames at the end of WWW addresses *are* case-sensitive. If you accidentally write http://www.myschool.edu/subjects instead of http://www.myschool.edu/Subjects you may not be able to reach your selected site. But if the address you want is http://www.MySchool.edu you will have no trouble reaching that site if you accidentally forget to capitalize the letters in the address (http://www.myschool.edu). Only the filenames after the edu or com portion of an address are case-sensitive.

Figuring out how to access a Web site of your choice is less obvious in Lynx, because there is no menu option for going to a new site visible on the screen. (You need to press **h** for help to get a list of Lynx commands.) No matter what location is currently on your screen, you can press **g** to "go to a specific URL."

When the line **URL to Open** appears at the bottom of the Lynx menu, type in the address of the location you want to reach. In figure 3.11, the URL for WebCrawler has been entered.

Creating and Adapting Bookmarks

Bookmarks let you save your favorite sites in a list so you can return to them easily. Rather than typing in long addresses each time you want to return to a site of your choice, all you do is open your bookmark file and click on your selected site.

Instead of relying exclusively on note cards and research notebooks to record information as you work on a research project, you may be able to use a Web browser to locate and then bookmark items you want to examine more carefully at a later time. You can create bookmarks for sources related to your area of investigation as well as to create collections of ref-

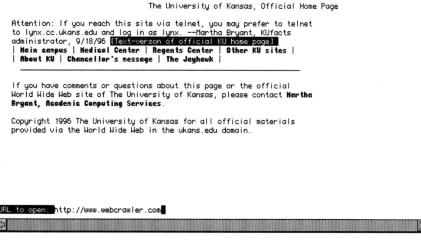

Figure 3.11   Opening a URL with Lynx.

erence tools such as almanacs and thesauri. You can also develop book-mark collections that include not only text-based content related to your topic, but also photos, illustrations, motion pictures, and recordings.

The technique for creating bookmarks varies from one browser to the next and from one version of a browser to another. To create a bookmark with Netscape 2.0, you first load a specific site. Then you click on **Add Bookmark.** With Lynx, you need to remember two commands: **a** (for add a site) and **v** (to view sites that have been bookmarked previously). When you press **a,** you will be asked if you want to download information or link to a site. If you want to create a link for your bookmark file, press **l.**

Figure 3.12 shows what a bookmark file looks like in Lynx.

Experiment with your bookmark file. It should become your personal launchpad to favorite Internet starting points. Include references that you think you will use often. Include your favorite search tools, too. If you create a separate bookmark file for each research project, you have easy access to the key Web sources you will need when you write your paper.

Some browsers such as Netscape allow you to create bookmarks with hierarchical lists of topics and subtopics (see figure 3.13). Other browsers,

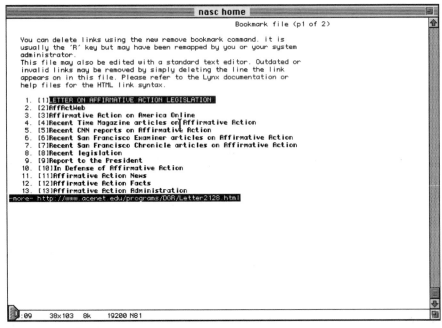

Figure 3.12   Bookmark file in Lynx.

such as Lynx, allow you to create only linear lists. You can, however, easily rename the default Lynx bookmark file—called lynx_bookmarks.html. For example, if you are an economics major, you can collect economics sites and then rename your file something like "economics.html." When you launch your browser, type **lynx_filename** instead of just typing **lynx.** Your customized bookmark file will appear on the screen. Each time you rename a file, you should delete the default file (lynx_bookmarks). The next time that you launch your Lynx program, you will have an empty bookmark file and can thus begin a new bookmark collection. By creating separate files for different topics, you can organize your information for easy retrieval. Chapter 8 provides you with more information on ways you can use bookmarks to organize the results of your searches.

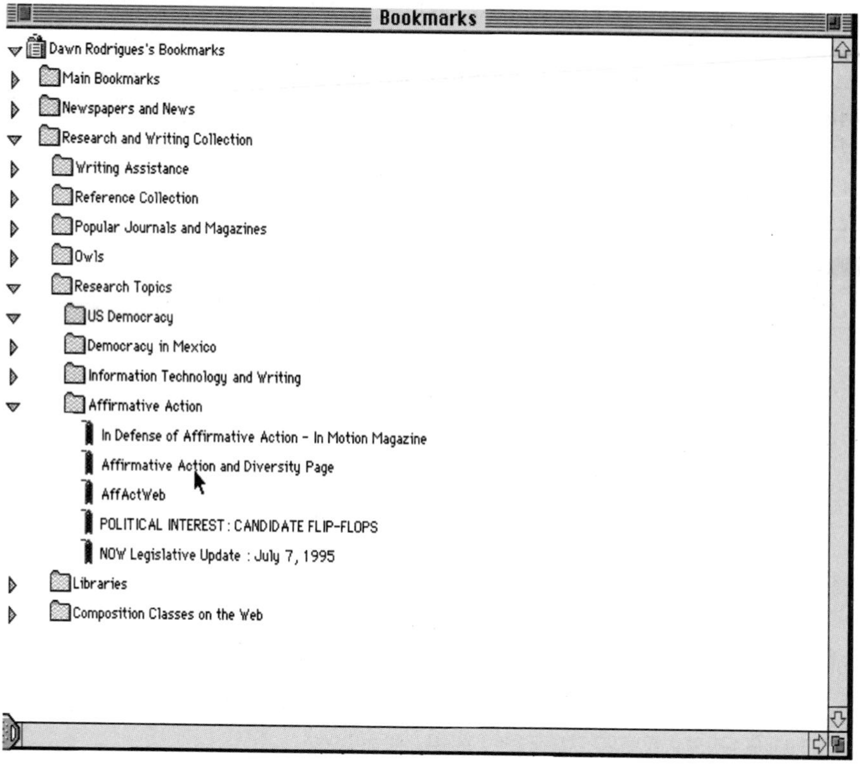

Figure 3.13   Hierarchical bookmarks in Netscape.

How do you create a set of bookmarks that suits your needs? Begin by using general subject-area collections on the Web or by using search engines to locate useful information. When you identify those sites that suit your needs, bookmark them. An individualized collection of sites is more helpful for your research needs than a set of reference sites that someone else has pieced together. An individualized collection of bookmarks is also an excellent starting point for a research project.

CONCLUSION

If you are new to the Internet, you may feel overwhelmed at first by the sea of information that's out there. Over time, however, as you develop the ability to find information and to create and organize bookmark files, you are likely to feel more secure navigating the Web from your own launch-points. If you develop expertise in locating useful information and in developing highly customized bookmark files such as personal reference collections, you'll begin to see the Web as a tool for research as well as an information resource.

END-OF-CHAPTER EXERCISES

1. In groups, use a different search engine to search for information on the same topic. Compare results and evaluate the search tools. Do different search engines generate different results? Bookmark sites that might be of interest to you or other students in your class who are planning to write on related topics.

2. After you have explored different search tools, add your favorites to your bookmark collections. If your browser allows you to create hierarchies, set up a subheading for favorite reference tools and another subheading for sites in your major. (Alternatively, turn your bookmark list into a reference home page. Just save your bookmarks and then open them from the file menu.)

3. Add several search engines or directories to your bookmark file. Discuss your reaction to these tools. How often do you think you might actually use them as you are working on a research project?

4. Select a topic (one that you could use for your next paper) and find ten valuable sites for researching that topic. Describe each source and evaluate its usefulness for your topic. Keep track of your search processes so that you can compare search strategies with classmates.

5. Come up with a list of possible research topics that different class members would be willing to work on together. Before the next class period, conduct a search on the topic assigned to your group. Use at least three different search engines. Keep track of the results. In class, compare the results of your search and the relative usefulness of the search engines you used.

SUGGESTIONS FOR RESEARCH AND WRITING

A current collection of sources related to these topics can be found at the Web site for this book.

1. A key problem in the information age is information explosion. People are drowning in a sea of information. With greater access to information, researchers have a new problem: how to determine which sources are worth using. Do a research project on information overload or on problems in validating sources. Are students and professionals coping? How? What are the issues?

2. This chapter introduced ways of surfing the Internet and techniques for bookmarking favorite sites. Is the Web's hypertext environment an advantage to some people and a disservice to others? Explore the issue of learning styles and Web navigation. You might do some research with your own class or with your colleagues at work. Are people with a propensity for a given learning style likely to gain Web savvy faster than others? Can technique overcome learning style? Determine whether effective organization of information helps people deal with a massive array of information on the Web.

CHAPTER 4

FINDING LIBRARIES ON THE WEB

The Internet makes it possible for you to access not only your own library's catalog, but also catalogs from libraries around the world. Why would you want to search other libraries? In some cases, you may need to locate essential sources on your topic that your library does not have. In other cases, you may want to read titles and abstracts just to get a sense of what has been published on your topic. Searching in several catalogs can help you focus your topic and determine your research strategies.

If you work with only a limited set of sources on a topic, you are not likely to develop a full and accurate understanding of the scope of your subject. Limiting yourself only to a chance grouping of articles or books that happen to be in your own college or university library prevents you from seeing the range of opinions that might be present elsewhere. Limiting yourself to the physical constraints of your own library's holdings doesn't enable you to do a good job as a researcher. Being aware of resources in your own library and throughout the world gives you an accurate sense of your options.

This chapter shows you how to move beyond your own library's home page to libraries everywhere. You'll learn how to access resources on library Web pages and in library catalogs worldwide. You'll discover that many resources listed on library Web pages are not traditional library sources at all; rather, they are links to Web sources equally useful for research.

FINDING THE LIBRARY OF YOUR CHOICE

You should locate the home page for the library of your choice and bookmark it for easy retrieval. Your library may be a hyperlink from the home page that loads when you launch your Internet browser. If not, you can find your library in other ways—by using a Web search tool to find your preferred library or by using one of the many library access sites, or lists of libraries, on the Web. Below you'll see how each of these procedures works.

Using a Search Tool to Locate Your Library

You can locate almost any college library quite easily with just a standard Web search tool. Here is an example of how to locate a library using Infoseek, one of the search tools described in chapter 3. Here's what you do:

1. Use NetSearch to locate Infoseek, one of the search engines you are presented with.
2. Click on Infoseek.
3. Type the name of the library of your choice in the search box, e.g., Williams College Library.
4. Click on the appropriate item in the list of search results.

Figure 4.1 shows results of that search.

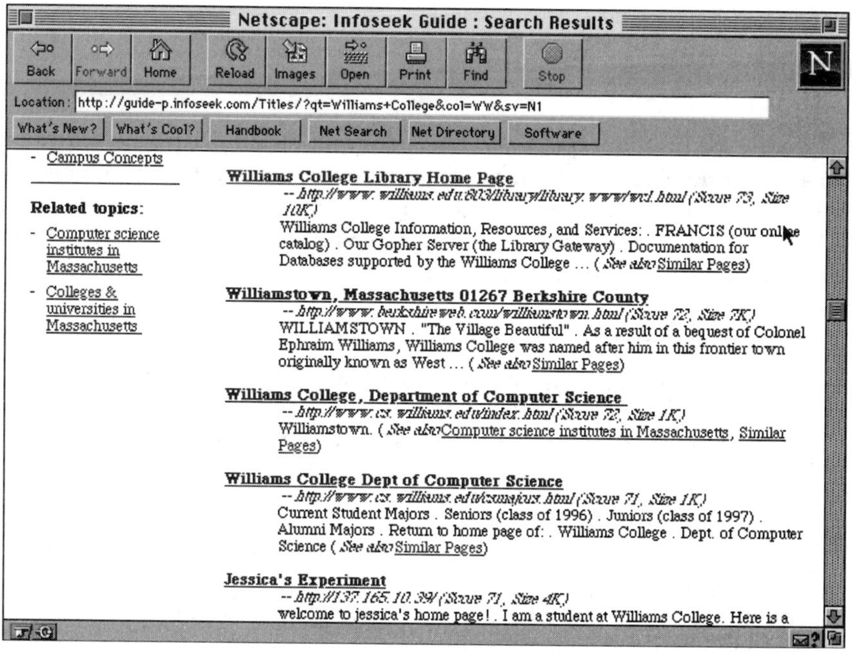

Figure 4.1   Infoseek search results for Williams College Library.

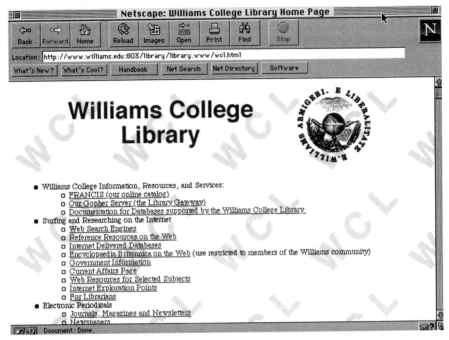

Figure 4.2   Williams College Library Home Page.

To go to the home page of the library, click on **Williams College Library Home Page.** Bookmark the page immediately. Figure 4.2 shows the Williams College Library Home Page.

From the home page, select **FRANCIS,** the online catalog at Williams. You should see the following message on your screen:

When you are connected, log in as library

Trying... Connected to FRANCIS.WILLIAMS.EDU, a DECSYSTEM-5000/200 running ULTRIX-4.2.
Connecting to FRANCIS, the Catalog of the Williams College Library

Type 'library' at the login prompt.

Please wait...

In a few moments (after a Telnet connection is launched by your computer) the following screen appears:

```
A > AUTHOR/NAME
T > TITLE
S > SUBJECT


C > CALL NO
G > GOVT DOC #

R > RESERVE Lists
B > CONNECT to another database

L > LIBRARY Information
V > VIEW your circulation record
```

At this point, you can begin searching in the Williams library catalog or press **L** for library information.

It would be wonderful if all library catalogs were alike. Unfortunately, different libraries use different cataloging software. Cataloging software was put into place long before the genesis of the Internet. Thus, as you explore the Web, you will need to learn different procedures for searching library catalogs. Librarians are hard at work developing common searching interfaces (see Z39.50 access later in this chapter).

Using a Library Access Site to Find Your Library

If your research requires you to use different online library catalogs, you should learn how to access libraries around the world in efficient ways. A useful way of finding the library of your choice is to use one of many sites that have sprung up on the Web where librarians have made available either lists of other libraries or software that enables you to find any library in the world. To use these access lists, you need to either know the address and type it into the location window of your browser or you need to use a search tool to locate the resource. Here's a list of particularly good resources. When you find one of these, be sure to bookmark it immediately. Should you want to delete it later, you can.

YaleInfo
gopher://libgopher.yale.edu:70/11/

Yale provides a special kind of Gopher service that handles the Telnet process behind the scenes. From Yale's Gopher, you choose a library and the Gopher telnets you directly to your selected location. The menu for all libraries in the United States is subdivided into menus for each state.

Libcat—Metronet
http://www.metronet.lib.mn.us:70/Oh/vendor/maven/lc/lcl.htm

Libcat offers hypertext links to more than a thousand libraries throughout the world. Information about each library includes special collection descriptions. Libcat also provides special instructions for each library catalog. You'll see options such as the following:

- The Online Catalog
- Library Gophers
- World Wide Web
- Special Collections
- Public Databases and Bibliographies

HYTELNET
http://library.usask.ca/hytelnet/

HYTELNET enables you to find the Telnet address of specific library catalogs and then, in many cases, merely click on the address to access the library of your choice. Its database includes campuswide information systems and library bulletin board systems at sites throughout the world. The opening screen is shown in Figure 4.3. From there, you'll find various lists of libraries such as the following:

Academic, Research, and General Libraries
Community College Libraries
Consortia
K–12 Libraries
Law Libraries
Medical Libraries
Public Libraries
United States

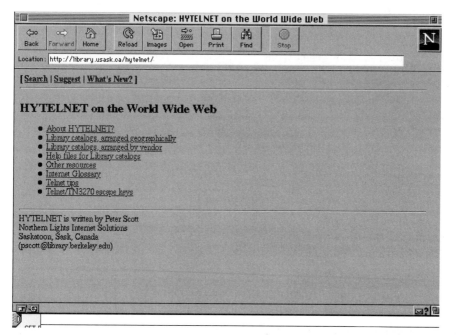

Figure 4.3   HYTELNET home page.

Inter-Links

http://www.nova.edu/Inter-Links/start.html

Inter-Links was created by Rob Kabacoff, Ph.D., from the Center for Psychological Studies at Nova Southeastern University in Fort Lauderdale, Florida. Selections from Inter-Links include these:

Full Text
- Books and Poetry
- Journals and Magazines

Card Catalogs
- Library Catalogs - Gopher
- Library Catalogs - HYTELNET

Literature Searches
- Search Book Titles - RLG
- Search Journal Titles - UnCover

Other Resources
- Florida Library Consortium
- Library of Congress Web
- Libraries with Web Interfaces
- Libcat: Library Resource Guide

Using YaleInfo to Locate a Library.   Try using one of the resources listed above, YaleInfo, to locate a library of your choice. When you locate the library you want, be sure to bookmark it for future reference. If, for example, you want to locate the Vanderbilt library, here's what you would do:

1. Type the following URL for YaleInfo into the location box of your browser:

   gopher://libgopher.cis.yale.edu

   At this point, a list of countries should appear on the screen.
2. From the list of countries available, select Americas

   gopher://libgopher.cis.yale.edu:70/11/Americas

3. From the next screen, select US.

   gopher://libgopher.cis.yale.edu:70/11/Americas/US

   A list of states should appear on your screen.
4. From the list of states, select Tennessee.
   The list of Tennessee libraries should appear on the next screen.
5. Select Vanderbilt.
   The Vanderbilt Central Library home page will appear on your screen (see figure 4.4).
6. Click on Acorn, the catalog of the Vanderbilt Libraries, to launch a Telnet connection and begin exploring the Vanderbilt library catalog.

PRACTICE BOX

1. There are many ways to locate libraries. Try using one or more of the sites listed in this chapter as starting points. If each group in your class explores one of the library launchpads, you can report results to one another, evaluating the benefits of different access points. Consider sending e-mail messages to your group. Or you can post messages to the Forum at the home page site for this book.

2. Explore several card catalogs, searching for a topic that you are considering for your research project. Note the problems you have with the different search interfaces. Which system do you prefer? Even though you are only doing preliminary searching, you may find some information that you would like to save. See chapter 8 for suggestions on how to take notes from electronic sources.

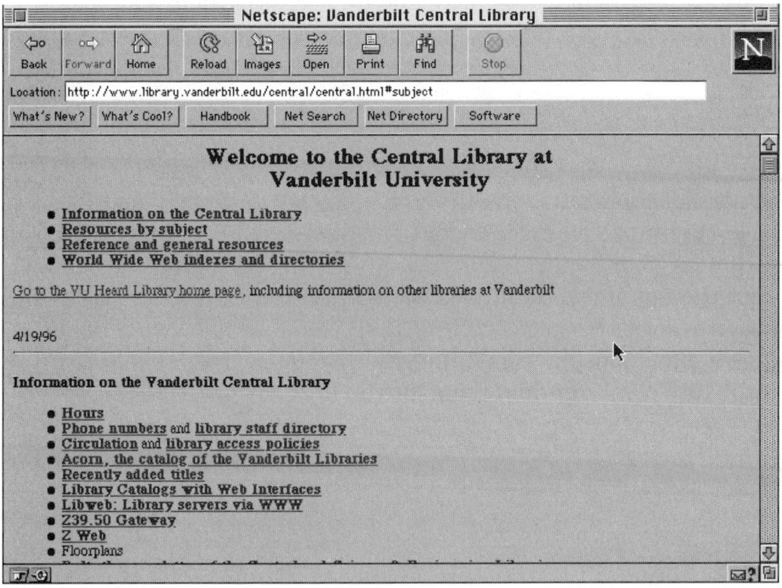

Netscape: Vanderbilt Central Library

Back | Forward | Home | Reload | Images | Open | Print | Find | Stop

Location: http://www.library.vanderbilt.edu/central/central.html#subject

What's New? | What's Cool? | Handbook | Net Search | Net Directory | Software

Welcome to the Central Library at Vanderbilt University

- Information on the Central Library
- Resources by subject
- Reference and general resources
- World Wide Web indexes and directories

Go to the VU Heard Library home page, including information on other libraries at Vanderbilt

4/19/96

Information on the Vanderbilt Central Library

- Hours
- Phone numbers and library staff directory
- Circulation and library access policies
- Acorn, the catalog of the Vanderbilt Libraries
- Recently added titles
- Library Catalogs with Web Interfaces
- Libweb: Library servers via WWW
- Z39.50 Gateway
- Z Web
- Floorplans

Figure 4.4   Vanderbilt Library home page.

Summary: How to Access a Library through the Web or the Internet

1. Find the library using a list of sites such as YaleInfo or another list of libraries.

2. When you locate the library of your choice, click to connect for Telnet access.

3. If the library has a Web-searchable interface, click to access the Web search screen.

4. If you need to Telnet directly, type in the Telnet address in your browser or use your Telnet application directly. Be sure that your computer is equipped with Telnet software.

DIFFERENT KINDS OF LIBRARY ACCESS

Libraries are in a state of transition as they move to the Web. Some colleges and universities now have Web-based searching available, but most still require you to connect to the library via a Telnet connection and then use the online catalog provided at the location. There are four different kinds of access: (1) Telnet access; (2) Web or Gopher interface access; (3) library catalog searching via Z39.50; and (4) access through catalogs with Web interfaces.

Telnet Access

Many libraries can be accessed only via Telnet. If you do not have a Telnet program accessible to you through your Web browser, you may have to learn how to launch an independent Telnet session. If you do have a Telnet program on your computer, you can type the Telnet address directly into the location window. Be sure to write down the login information, for sometimes it will not be on the screen when you need it. (A word of advice: Although most systems have an online help program available to you, you should probably print out directions for the libraries you use regularly.)

Web or Gopher Interface Access

Many libraries have a Web or a Gopher interface. Through a Web or Gopher area for their library, librarians can offer their clients much information about the library and the services it provides along with access to the catalog itself.

A list of libraries with Gopher interfaces is available at this address:

Peripatetic Gopher Libraries List
gopher://peg.cwis.uci.edu:7000/11/gopher.welcome/peg/LIBRARIES

A list of libraries with Web interfaces is available at this address:

Libweb: Library Servers via WWW
http://sunsite.berkeley.edu/Libweb/

Having a Web or Gopher interface doesn't mean that the interface for the library catalog is based on Gopher or the Web. What it usually means is that the library has developed a page of useful information and links, one of which happens to be a Telnet link to the library. Somewhere

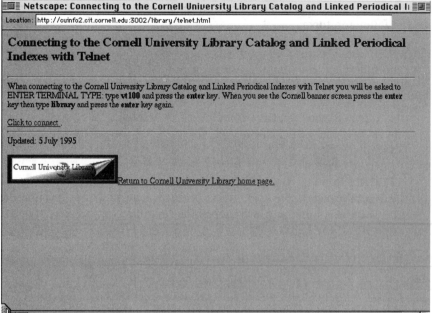

Figure 4.5   Telnet link from Cornell University Library home page.

on each library home page you will be directed to click to enter the cata-log. Typically, this means that when you select this link, your system launches a Telnet session to enable you to log in to the remote library cat-alog. At this writing, Cornell's library is accessed via a Telnet link from the Cornell home page (see figure 4.5).

Z39.50 Access

When you move from library to library, you will discover that some catalogs are quite different from others. You'll need to use different com-mands in different library catalogs to search for subjects, titles, and authors. If, for example, you've learned how to use the MELVYL system (in California), you'll discover that the same commands for searching do not work with Harvard's HOLLIS system.

To solve the interface problem—the problem of having to learn many different ways of searching—librarians have been working on a standard method of catalog design. They have organized their catalogs in a way that enables the entire collection to be included in a Wide Area Information System (WAIS) database using what is called the Z39.50 protocol. WAIS is a program for searching specific collections of information that have been developed and stored on a special computer. The Z39.50 standard searches use the following form:

FIND <index name> <search terms>

The following are common index names:

au author search

ti title search

to topic search (Dartmouth only)

su subject search (Harvard only)

Examples:

FIND AU Twain

FIND TI Dune

FIND SU Space

The DISPLAY command will display the results.

Type HELP for help.

When you search from a site that offers Z39.50 searching, you can search many libraries' collections using the same search procedures.

Figure 4.6 shows an opening screen for Z39.50 access. This web site

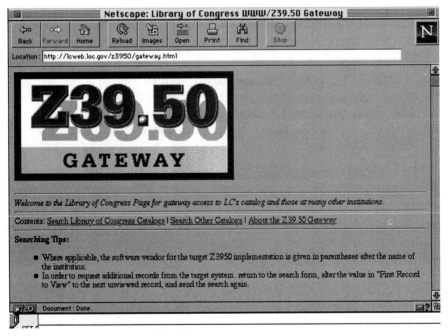

Figure 4.6   Opening screen for Z39.50 access.

provides access to the Library of Congress collection. It also provides a hypertext list of the following Z39.50 access points:

United States Naval Academy, Annapolis (INNOPAC)
University of Arizona (INNOPAC)
University of Arkansas, Little Rock (DRA)
University of California—MELVYL System
University of California, San Francisco (INNOPAC)
University of Iowa (NOTIS)
University of Illinois, Urbana (NOTIS)

Although the Z39.50 search screens at different locations vary slightly in format, they all look something like this:

UNIVERSITY OF CALIFORNIA (MELVYL) Z39.50 SEARCH FORM

First Record to View: 1__ Maximum Records to Retrieve: 190_

Select Database to be Searched:[TEN]

Key to Databases:
 * CAT - All Bibliographic Records (approximately 8 million)
 * TEN - Last 10 Years of CAT Database (approx. 1.5 million records)
 * PE - Periodicals Database (approximately 800,000 titles)

Enter Term 1: affirmative _____
[Subject_____][Word____]

(*)AND ( )OR ( )AND NOT

Enter Term 2: action_____
(*)AND ( )OR ( )AND NOT
(*)AND ( )OR ( )AND NOT

Enter Term 3: _____
[Subject_____][Phrase__]

Submit Query Clear Form

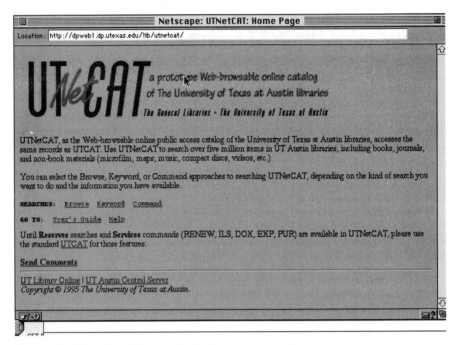

Figure 4.7   University of Texas at Austin Library search screen.

Catalogs with Web Interfaces

Even easier than using the Z39.50 interface is searching a catalog with its own Web interface. As more libraries develop Web catalogs, everyone's research life will be less complicated. The University of Texas at Austin is one of a growing list of libraries providing this kind of service. Notice the easy-to-use search screen in figure 4.7.

EXPLORING THE LIBRARY OF CONGRESS WEB SITE

The Library of Congress is taking an active role in Internet and World Wide Web development. The collection includes links to exhibits and events and access to special collections such as the American Memory Project and to the Library of Congress's book collection. Understanding this site can help you comprehend the current state of library catalogs and the degree to which their holdings can be made available through the Web.

The Library of Congress showcases its collections on its Web site and also provide links to libraries' collections at other sites. The address for the Library of Congress World Wide Web site is http://lcWeb.loc.gov/.

From the Library of Congress Home Page, scroll down to "Library of Congress Online Services." The Library of Congress's Web interface is only the top layer of services. To use either MARVEL (the Machine-Assisted Realization of the Virtual Electronic Library) or LOCIS (Library of Congress Information System), where you can search the catalog, you first make your selection on the Web page. Then you are connected to either a Gopher system for MARVEL or to the LOCIS. Figure 4.8 shows the Library of Congress page with access to MARVEL and LOCIS system via Telnet.

Note that MARVEL is an information server that uses a Gopher system. LOCIS uses proprietary online cataloging software. Figure 4.9 shows what the MARVEL screen looks like in Netscape. Figure 4.10 shows the LOCIS screen.

In addition to using the LOCIS catalog to find books and periodicals on your topic, you may want to use it to access the Library of Congress Subject Headings. If you select Library of Congress Subject Headings from

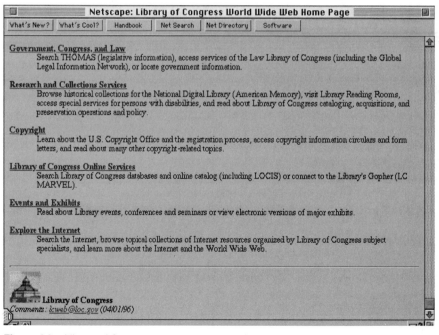

Figure 4.8 Library of Congress page.

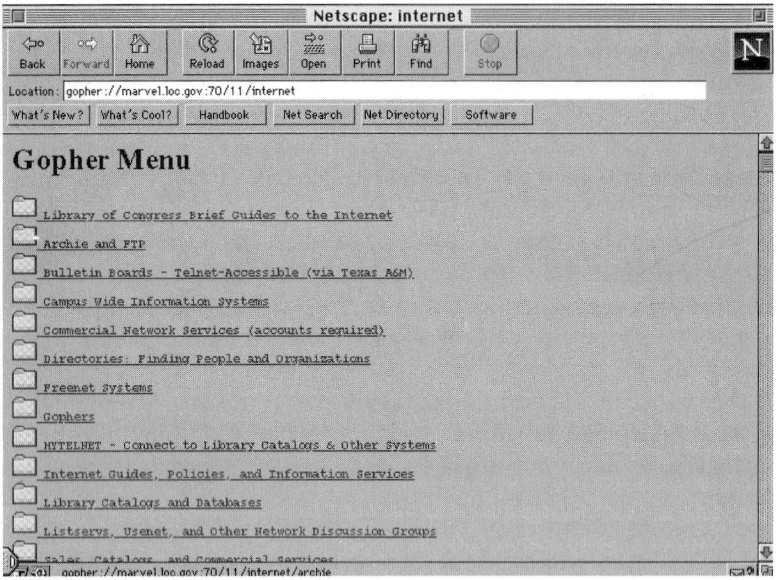

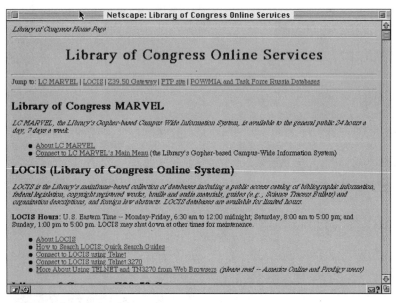

Figure 4.9   MARVEL screen in Netscape.

Figure 4.10   LOCIS screen.

the LOCIS menu, you will get several choices. Select #6 if you want to look up a subject heading for your topic.

LOCIS: Library of Congress Information System

1 BOOKS: English language books 1968-, French 1973-, German,   LOCI
   Portuguese, Spanish 1975-, other European languages 1976-77,
   non-European languages 1978-79. Some microforms 1984-.

2 BOOKS earlier than the dates above. Some serials, maps,   PREM
   music, audiovisual items.

3 Combination of files 1 and 2 above (LOCI and PREM).

4 SERIALS cataloged at LC & some other libraries since 1973.   LOCS

5 MAPS and other cartographic items cataloged at LC 1968-   LOCM
   and some other research libraries 1985-. Atlases (which
   are books) are in LOCI and PREM.

6 SUBJECT TERMS and cross references from LC Subject Headings.   LCXR

12 Return to LOCIS MENU screen.

LOCIS does not provide 24-hour access. If you get used to using the Library of Congress Subject Headings online through LOCIS, you should realize that you won't be able to access them during certain hours. Don't be surprised when you get a "connection refused" message. At the time of this writing, LOCIS operating hours are (U.S. Eastern Time) Monday-Friday, 6:30 A.M. to 12:00 midnight; Saturday, 8:00 A.M. to 5:00 P.M.; and Sunday, 1:00 P.M. to 5:00 P.M. LOCIS may shut down at other times for maintenance.

GUIDEBOOKS ON LIBRARY ACCESS

Another way you can learn about libraries across the world and how to access them is by using one of several guidebooks that are available on the Web. Some university librarians have authored excellent guidebooks for accessing library catalogs from remote sites. Two of the most useful are *Accessing On-Line Bibliographic Databases* (or *Barron's Guide)* and *Nysernet's New User's Guide.* These are excellent resources to acquire if you want to learn more about other libraries. Below you will learn about these guides and about some of the resources described in them.

Barron's Guide

Billy Barron and Marie-Christine Mahe's *Accessing On-Line Biblio-graphic Databases* is available from the Yale library at gopher://yale-info.yale.edu. (As noted earlier, to reach a Gopher on the Web, just type the address in the same box you would type an "http" address. The http indicates that your address is a hypertext transfer protocol site—in other words, a Web site. When you begin your address with "gopher," you are indicating that your address is a Gopher site.) This guide includes directions for logging in to libraries but does not actually connect you. For example, directions for accessing the JANET collection in the United Kingdom are given as follows:

Telnet to uk.ac.nsfnet-relay

Once connected you will be prompted for the address of a host. Enter the Internet address (either name or numeric) at this point.

Specify your terminal type when prompted (probably vt100).

Nysernet's New User's Guide

An Internet library guide worth getting is Nysernet's *New User's Guide to Useful and Unique Resources on the Internet* (ftp:// nysernet.org). Among the libraries included in this guide are the CARL system and the New York Public Library System. Some of the unusual Web resources described in this guide include the following: The General Accounting Office Reports Archive; Music on the Net: Lyric and Discography Archive; and Project Hermes: U.S. Supreme Court Opinions.

The CARL System (http://www.carl.org/Welcome.html).   The Colorado Alliance of Research Libraries is a consortium of universities, colleges, and schools that use the same cataloging system and set of databases, known as CARL. In addition to making it easier to search multiple libraries, an advantage of the CARL system is that the record of "hits" that your search tool produces in one library can be carried through to as many system libraries as you wish. When you have exhausted the information resources in one system you merely "switch databases" and search another. The databases include 39 libraries (as of this writing) and other databases such as the Book Review Index, UnCover, and the Librarian's Yellow Pages. A noteworthy feature of the CARL system is the Quick Search, which allows you to enter search commands any time in your research without returning to the main menu. An even more interesting feature is Express Search. Express Search allows you to use features from a "hit" you have retrieved in a search for similar records. When you enter **X** for Express Search, you are presented with a screen that shows the original records you found organized into call number, author, and other entries. Each of these items is numbered so that you can select the line number of the item you want to use as the starting point for a new search based on terms related to this record. Here is an example:

WELCOME TO EXPRESS SEARCH
Following are the call number and other entries found in the previous record. Pick the number of the term you would like to search and the search will be performed automatically.

CALL NUMBER: (Materials shelved nearby)
1. LC4031 S25 1990

AUTHOR(s): (Materials by or about the same author)
2. Salend, Spencer J.

OTHER ENTRIES (Materials on similar topics)
3. Handicapped children Education United States
4. Mainstreaming in education United States
5. Alphabetical List of Entries

Enter line number for search (Q to Quit)>3

HANDICAPPED 3366 ITEMS
HANDICAPPED + CHILDREN 1349 ITEMS
patience—EDUCATION is a long one. . .
HANDICAPPED + CHILDREN + EDUCATION 967 ITEMS
patience—UNITED is a long one. . .
HANDICAPPED + CHILDREN + EDUCATION + UNITED 591 ITEMS
patience—STATES is a long one. . .
HANDICAPPED + CHILDREN + EDUCATION + UNITED + STATES 591 ITEMS

For the 591 items that have

HANDICAPPED + CHILDREN + EDUCATION + UNITED + STATES
Press <RETURN> or type <Q> for a new search.

Enter N for Name search
W for WORD search
B to BROWSE by title, call number, or series
S to STOP or SWITCH to another database

There is also a quick search—type QS for details or Type ? For new information about searching
ENTER COMMAND>>

NYPLnet: The New York Public Library Online Catalog (http://gopher.nypl.org). If you want to know what the New York Public Library has on your topic, you can learn how to access and search it. Here is a list of databases available to you:

1. NYPL Branch Libraries Catalog
2. Metropolitan Inter-Library Cooperative System Regional Catalog
3. NYPL Dance Collection Catalog

Unusual Web Resources

The General Accounting Office Reports Archive
(ftp://try.cu.nih.gov)

General Accounting Office reports are available over the Internet. Sample reports include: Computer Security: Government-Wide Planning Process Had Limited Impact; Drug-Exposed Infants: A Generation at Risk; and Home Visiting: A Promising Early Intervention Strategy.

Music on the Net: Lyric and Discography Archive
(ftp://wacs.uwp.edu)

This archive of lyrics includes songs from popular as well as classical artists. It is located at the University of Wisconsin-Parkside. You can find a musical telephone directory address list and a list of musical mailing lists (ftp://vacs.uwp.edu:/pub/music/misc/mail.lists.music).

Project Hermes: U.S. Supreme Court Opinions
(ftp://cwru.edu)

U.S. Supreme Court opinions have been made available by Case Western Reserve University. Each opinion includes concurring and dissenting opinions. Project Hermes began in 1990. The objective of the project was to make copies of the Court's opinions immediately available in electronic form. For record keeping, the GAO asks that those who use this Internet service send an e-mail address to kh3@cu.nih.gov.

CONCLUSION

Although it is already possible to search many libraries at once, with librarians hard at work and funded by several major government grants, expect improvements. Realize that the way you search for information today will not be the way you search for information next year. In a recent article in *The Chronicle of Higher Education* ("Researchers Temper their Ambitions for Digital Libraries," Nov. 24, A19), Robert L. Jacobson writes about librarians' efforts to develop better ways of searching many libraries' collections. He explains that librarians have determined that developing standards to satisfy all ages and ability levels of their patrons will not be easy. They have decided to work in two parts: at one level they will try to come up with a generalized approach, a design that will help most users most of the time; on another level, they will attempt to create a more sophisticated approach for advanced users. If you use the Web regularly to explore library collections, you'll be able to watch new developments taking place almost daily.

END-OF-CHAPTER EXERCISES

1. Once a library has a card catalog on the Internet, the next step is usually to put library information on the network, too. Such information as hours, policies, and collection information is standard. From there, libraries across the country provide vastly different resources. Find the following libraries and examine the range of information they provide to patrons: Rutgers, Cornell, University of Michigan.

   What kind of information is most helpful? Is any of this information useful to you even though you are not a student at the school whose Web page you are using? If you find valuable information, you can save it to disk. (Check the directions included on your browser's menu bar under **File.**)

2. Collect a list of libraries that might be useful to you or to students in your class or in your major and bookmark them so that you can refer to them easily. You might want to find different kinds of libraries. Here are a few specialized libraries. See if you can identify more.

- Rutgers University Law Library (has useful links to Internet law)

  URL: http://www.rutgers.edu/lawschool.html

- Michigan State University: Vincent Voice Library

  URL: http://web.msu.edu/vincent/index.html

- Cornell University Engineering Library: ICE (Internet Connections for Engineering)

  URL: http://www.englib.cornell.edu/ice/ice-index.html

SUGGESTIONS FOR RESEARCH
AND WRITING

A current collection of sources related to these topics can be found at the Web site for this book.

1. Reading and writing processes are changing in the information age. Explore the shift from a print-based to a digital age. To what extent are librarians coping? Examine the Digital Library Project, a collaboration amongst several research universities, to learn about research in creating digital collec-

tions. Explore ways newspapers have moved to the Web. What kinds of transformations take place when periodicals move to the Web? What kinds of new media have emerged (e.g., e-zines, e-journals, etc.)? What are the chief problems developers are encountering? How are patrons coping? Is access to Web terminals an issue?

2. The U.S. Commerce Department has been especially interested in preserving open access to information. They have funded grants to develop Web projects in libraries, hospitals, and nursing homes. To what extent have they been successful? You might want to explore several projects by finding their sites on the Web and doing e-mail interviews with project leaders. Are community members using the Web to learn about events in their area? Are businesses providing information to their clients?

CHAPTER 5

FINDING LIBRARY RESOURCES ON THE WEB

Many newcomers to the Web wonder whether they can find the same resources on the Internet that they are familiar with in libraries, that is, books, periodicals, periodical indexes, and newspapers. The answer is, "It depends." You can find newspapers, abstracts, and references, and even a free encyclopedia, on the Web. But you can't access copyrighted databases such as Social Sciences and Humanities Index or LEXIS-NEXIS unless your campus has purchased them for network use. You can locate books and, in some cases, check them out over the Web and even have them delivered to you. But except for those that are out of copyright or sample chapters of recent books that have been made available by publishers, you can't read most books online.

At many schools, you can process interlibrary loan orders through the Web. You need to discover what's available at your college or community library. Only by devoting time to exploring your library and its Web resources as well as the free resources available to everyone on the Web can you determine the best ways to integrate library and Web in your own research projects.

LIBRARY OFFERINGS ON THE WEB

Much depends on your local contexts and the degree to which your library has migrated toward the Web. The main difference between one Web and Internet library site and another is the number of copyrighted databases and other proprietary information that a school makes available to its students. Some college and company libraries provide not only access to indexes, but also full-text access to a wide variety of journals. Even if your library does not have the database you need, you may be able to use the

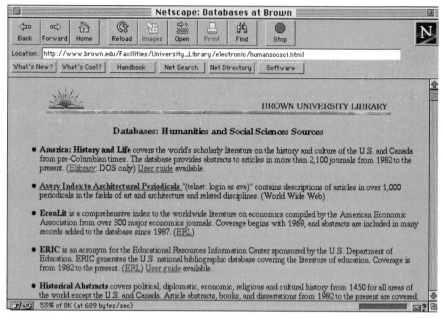

Figure 5.1   Databases available at Brown University.

Web to locate a library that does subscribe to that database and then drive to the library and access the database there. Figure 5.1 shows the list of databases available at Brown University. The list includes ERIC (described later in the section Indexes and Abstracts) which, though available in a subscription service, is also available free at some Internet sites.

Despite differences in access to copyrighted databases, everyone has access to the free resources on the Web. Fortunately, with the explosion of interest in the Web, more and more free resources are being developed, some by librarians. Many libraries offer locally developed materials such as subject bibliographies and reference guides. For example, the Stanford Library has many reference collections, including one to help researchers in African American Studies. The library staff explains that their site

> contains many titles on the historical and contemporary experience of African Americans, making it an excellent place for students conducting research in this area. Because of the interdisciplinary nature of African American Studies, relevant titles are often dispersed throughout the general collection depending upon subject matter.

Similar collections can be found all over the Web, and you don't need to be a student at each respective college or university to access public information resources such as these. If your home library doesn't have the kind of information you need, the trick is to find another library that does and then bookmark your find so that you can access it later.

Since different libraries have different specialties, you should shop around to find a library that happens to have a good collection of information or other resources in your field. For example, the Colorado State University Library lists abstracts in different subject areas at its Gopher site. The Columbia University Library (www.cc.columbia.edu/libraries) includes pointers to reserve listings for courses all over the world at its Electronic Reserves Clearinghouse (http://www.cc.columbia.edu/~rosedale/). The Rutgers University Library (www.rutgers.edu/rulib) has an excellent collection of databases in British and American history.

Along with hypertext links to the library catalog, the Rutgers University Library Home Page (see figure 5.2) points to collections of resources in different disciplines (Arts and Humanities; Social Sciences, Business, and Law; etc.). Clicking on one of these areas leads you to a selection of resources from library materials, CD-ROM databases, and Web sites for that area. For instance, if you select Arts and Humanities, your screen will display a collection of both library and Web sites for the the arts and humanities, one selection of which is American and British History. Select-

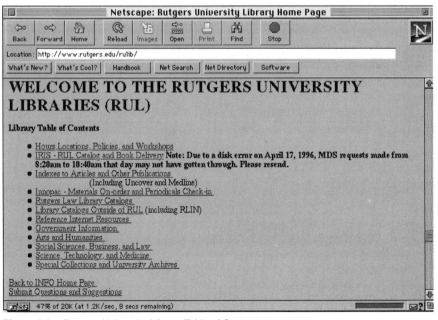

Figure 5.2   Rutgers University Library Table of Contents.

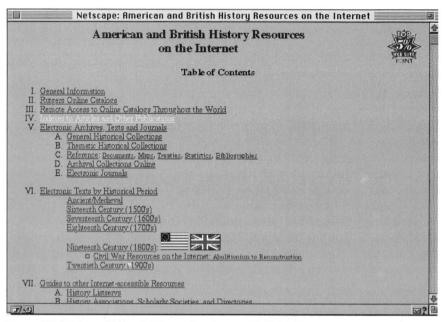

Figure 5.3   Rutgers University Library American and British history page.
Copyright 1996 Netscape Communications Corp. All rights reserved. This page may not be reprinted or copied without the express written permission of Netscape.

ing American and British History leads you to the page displayed in figure 5.3. These resource collections are a fine example of how librarians are helping researchers learn how to integrate library and Web in their research.

PRACTICE BOX

1. What CD-ROM databases are available to you in your library? on the Web?

2. Examine three of these databases. Compare search strategies. Which is the hardest to use? Which is easiest?

3. Work with several classmates on a common topic. Together, see what kinds of Internet sources you can find on your topic. Next, see what sources are available in a CD-ROM database. Keep a record of your search strategies.

4. Compare your results. Which sources of information were the most productive for your topic? How many of these sources were in proprietary databases?

TRADITIONAL LIBRARY RESOURCES ON THE WEB

Many traditional kinds of resources are available on the Web: books, periodicals, periodical indexes and other indexes, encyclopedias and other references, and newspapers. Some of these online sources are digitized versions of their print counterparts, whereas other sources are hypertext publications that were created specifically for the Web and are not available in print. The following box should help you get an overall sense of the relationship betweenWeb resources and library resources.

What's on the Web? What's in the Library?

	Library	*Web*
Books	Yes	Provides access to library catalogs where you can locate books on your topic. Provides full-text access to out-of-copyright books such as those in the Project Gutenberg collection. Provides access to selected chapters of some books (offered by publishing companies at their sites).
Periodicals	Yes	Many full-text journal articles are now available by searching proprietary databases on the Web. New electronic journals are also available.
Periodical indexes	Yes (both paper and CD-ROM)	Online indexes are available on the Web to campus communities that have subscribed to the services. UnCover, a periodical index with delivery service available for a fee, can be used to locate journal articles on your topic. Such full-text periodical indexing services as the Electric Library and NlightN offer trial subscriptions.

Encyclopedias	Yes (print and online)	*Encyclopaedia Britannica* is now widely available. Check with your reference librarian. Subscriptions are available to individuals. Free Internet Encyclopedia is now available on the Web.
References	Yes	Those no longer in copyright are on the Web: *Roget's Thesaurus, Bartlett's Quotations,* etc.
Search tools	Online catalogs and other databases	Web now offers many search tools. Online Computer Library Center now offers searches of Web and library to subscribers. Individual libraries provide access to online catalogs.
Newspapers	CD-ROM databases in many libraries	Free access to most newspapers on the Web. Registration required for *The New York Times* and some other newspapers.
Government documents	Yes	Typically free on the Web.
Digital museums, field trips, digitized special collections of maps, pictures, journals, etc.	Limited. Special collections in individual libraries sometimes include journals and pictures.	Many collections of images, including digitized versions of valuable hand-written maps and manuscripts, have been developed. (For example, see the American Memory project at the Library of Congress.)

Books on the Web

You can "enter" libraries around the world and explore the collections through Internet or Web connections. Along with out-of-copyright books available at such sites as Project Gutenberg and Internet Wiretap, you'll find some recent books available on the Web. In addition, check publishers' Web sites to see if they are providing access to selected chapters of new books; a growing practice is to offer an occasional chapter or so to give readers a sense of what the book is about. In addition, most book publishers now have Web sites that allow you to search their catalogs.

Some book publishers specialize in online books. For instance, at the On-line Books Page (http://www.cs.cmu.edu/Web/books.html) you'll find an index of online books and book projects alongside pointers to current books that are for sale. One noteworthy online book project accessible from this site is the National Academy Press (NAP), an organization created by the National Academy of Sciences to publish the reports issued by the National Academy of Sciences, the National Academy of Engineering, the Institute of Medicine, and the National Research Council. At the NAP On-Line Book Store, you can order books online, search for titles, or browse through the catalog. You can even "shop" for books:

> For your convenience you may pick up a shopping basket. The shopping basket gives you the freedom to roam around the bookstore, pick up books, and then decide which books you would like to purchase. The books in your shopping basket remain there until you decide to purchase them or put them back on the shelf.

> For the casual browser, we offer an Express Checkout option that lets you purchase a book at a time. You DO NOT need to register for this service.

Project Bartleby: The Public Library of the Internet

http://www.cc.columbia.edu/acis/bartleby/

This collection of publicly available hypertext books includes a search engine. You can scan a book and locate the passages that might have relevance to your topic. Books in this collection include the following: Strunk, William, Jr. 1918. *The Elements of Style;* Melville, Herman. 1853. *Bartleby the Scrivener: A Story of Wall Street;* Inaugural Addresses of the Presidents of the United States, 1989.

Similar collections are available at the following locations:

- Electronic Text Center (University of Virginia)
- Project Gutenberg
  + Via master FTP server at University of Illinois, Urbana-Champaign (UIUC)
  + Via Web site at UIUC
- Humanities Text Initiative (at UMichigan)
- Internet Wiretap book collection
- Oxford Text Archive
- Etext.org archives (lots of e-zines and shorter or unpublished etexts)
- Book Stacks Library

- Samizdat Express (eclectic collection of texts and pointers)
- Links to Electronic Book and Text Sites (from OmniMedia)

NovelList Electronic Readers' Advisory
http://www.carl.org/nlhome.html

This fee-based service provides readers with information about new books that have been published on topics of interest to them—based on a registration form that new users fill out.

Bookstores on the Web

You can find bookstores on the Web. Internet Road Map to Books provides you with the following list of sites:

BOOKSELLERS' WWW PAGES
- American Booksellers Association
- Antiquarian Booksellers' Association of America
- Virtual Booksellers Association
- Booksellers directories, from BookWire and the Internet Book Fair

ONLINE EDITIONS OF BOOKS
- Web editions from Bookport
- Adobe Acrobat editions from Dial-a-Book
- Various editions from the On-Line Book Store

Periodicals, Magazines, and Online Journals on the Web

It may be some time before most of the journals you need to access for your research needs make their way to the free Internet. Why? Even though it would be less expensive for journals to publish on the Web instead of in print, Web publication is still not seen as similarly prestigious in most circles. And even though electronic journals can be distributed internationally in an instant, many researchers are reluctant to publish their work in these journals. The journals that seem to be succeeding on the Web are those that publish both an online and a print version. One such journal is the *Journal of Artificial Intelligence Research* (gopher://p.gp.cs.cmu.edu/). Rob Kling's article explains why this journal is succeeding:

Each article is formatted and paginated as it would appear in a printed journal. Someone who prints the Postscript file has an article which looks like the photocopy of an article from a traditional p-journal [print journal]. A publishing house, Morgan-Kaufman, also sells a printed version of the journal in an annual issue to libraries and others . . . calming authors' fears of publishing stigmatized electronic medium because it always looks like a p-journal and can be purchased in paper form.

Ron Kling and Lisa Covi. Special Issue on Electronic Journals and
Legitimate Media in the Systems of Scholarly Publishing.
The Information Society, 1995. Available:
http://www.ics.uci.edu/~kling/klingej2.html

Here are some periodical areas on the Web:

Electronic Journals and Journal Information

http://www.lib.uchicago.edu/LibInfo/Libraries/Chemistry/cgimail-
.html

This list was prepared by a chemistry librarian at the University of Chicago. It includes links to both online journals in chemistry and print journals. Links to sites with full text are identified in the list. (Note: Proprietary journals require a password.)

Electronic Journal collection from CICnet

gopher://gopher.cic.net:2000/11/e-serials

The CIC is the academic consortium of the members of the Big Ten athletic conference and the University of Chicago. The CIC-EJC is a collaborative initiative between the librarians of the CIC member universities, CICnet, and the CIC Center. Some collectons of online journals and magazines included are listed below:

COLLECTIONS

- Electronic Journal Collection from CICnet
- E-Zines -Electronic Magazines
- E-Zines -A New Source
- E-Zines -Useful, but unsupported
- Newspapers, Magazines, & Newsletters

FEATURED

- Academe -Chronicle of Higher Education
- CMC Magazine -Computer Mediated Communication
- EDUCOM -Educational Technology

- Electronic Newstand -Samples
- IBC Journal -Book Reviews
- InterText Magazine -Fiction
- Journal of Statistical Education
- Multiworld Magazine
- Time Warner Magazines -Samples
- ZiffNet Computer Magazines -Samples

University of California-San Diego

http://gort.ucsd.edu/newjour/

Archive of journal announcements, with links to Internet locations. Dates back to August 1993. More than 1,000, ranging from literary journals to cultural magazines. The journals can be searched with keywords. When you search for a journal, you get a summary of its scope and a pointer to its Internet location.

Electronic Journals

gopher://bubl.bath.ac.uk:7070/11/BUBL_Main_Menu/

This list of e-journals from the BUBL site is fairly comprehensive. If you select "Link to Major Electronic Journal Sites" you'll get a list of journals to choose from, including the following:

Electronic Newsstand
Red Rock Eater News Service Archive
Scholarly Communications Project Electronic Journals
Scientist Newsletter, The
Social Science Journals & Newsletters
Springer-Verlag Journals & Publications
WIRED Online Gopher

Zines from the Umich E-Text Archive

gopher://etext.archive.umich.edu/11/Zines/

gopher://etext.archive.umich.edu/11/Zines-by-subject

This is a totally uncensored, unedited list of "zines"—computer magazines that anyone can create and publish online. You'll find an array of zines, including *Practical Nutrition, Breakaway* (a discussion of Marxism), and *Computer News.*

Inter-Links Journals List
http://www.nova.edu/Inter-Links/start.html

Interlinks is a project of Nova Southeastern University. Most links provide information about the journals listed, not full-text access to them. A portion of the list of e-journals in this collection follows:

Architronic: Electronic Journal of Architecture
Botanical Electronic News
Bryn Mawr Classical Review
Bryn Mawr Medieval Review
Bulletin of the American Mathematical Society (New Series)
Chronicle of Higher Education
CLIONET: the Australian Electronic Journal of History
Current Cites
DargonZine
Education, Research and Perspectives
Electronic Antiquity: Communicating the Classics
Electronic Journal of Analytic Philosophy
Electronic Journal on Virtual Culture
Ethnomusicology Digest
Flora Online: Journal for Collections-Oriented Botanical Research
EASI's Information Technology and Disabilities (journal)
Internet Monthly Report
Interpersonal Computing and Technology (The IPCT-J Electronic Journal)
Jewish Studies Judaica eJournal
Journal of Artificial Intelligence Research
Journal of Fluids Engineering DATABANK (ISSN 0098-2202)
Journal of Political Ecology
Journal of Statistics Education
Journal of Technology Education (ISSN 1045-1064)
Journal of World Anthropology

PRACTICE BOX

1. Examine several booksellers' or publishers' areas on the Web, looking for information on your topic but also noticing the way each company has designed its electronic area. What is the most appealing electronic bookstore you can find? the least appealing? Why?

2. Many journals are being printed in two ways—print and online. Some journals are being developed exclusively for the Web and thus have hypertext organization. While searching for information for your current research project, examine different journals, noting the different ways they are formatted (see URLs for journals in this section). Share examples of the following: the most innovatively designed Web journal; the most old-fashioned Web journal; the most readable Web journal.

3. Review some old terms and learn some new ones. First the old terms. Look up the definition of the following: **periodical, serial, magazine.** Now the new terms. Explore several online journals and see if you can distinguish between the following: **e-journal, e-zine, zine, online journal.**

Note: Trying to find a definition of an e-journal may be difficult. For starters, think of electronic journals as moderated periodicals distributed either regularly or irregularly in an electronic format, typically through a computer network. Moderated implies that the publication is subject to editorial control. Examine several e-journals and see if they fit this definition.

Indexes and Abstracts

Traditionally, the main value of periodical indexes is to help you locate articles on your topic. With full texts beginning to be available, periodical indexes allow you to skim the articles before deciding whether or not to save to disk or print.

Although most full-text services are only available to you if your school or place of employment subscribes to the service, there are a few services that offer free trials (e.g., Electric Library and NlightN). You can explore these services and see if they are worth your consideration. The search returns full text of articles in major academic journals. Options allow you to search only in newspapers or in television transcripts.

You can find many periodical sources by searching in library catalogs that index both books and periodicals. One of the most useful indexes to periodicals, UnCover, allows you to search free (ignore repeated requests to include your credit card number). Another free resource you won't want to ignore is ERIC—the Educational Resources Information Center (see figure 5.4).

UnCover
http://hplus.harvard.edu/alpha/CARL.html

telnet://128.103.151.247:3015/

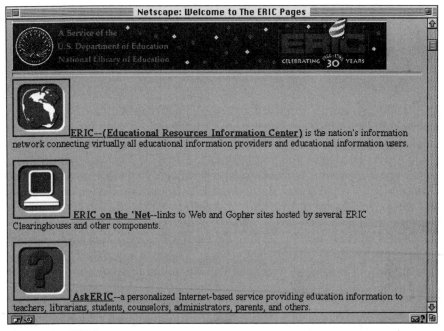

Figure 5.4   ERIC home page.

UnCover is a periodical index database and a delivery system with more than 17,000 titles. As journals are received by CARL, the tables of contents are immediately added to the database. The primary benefit to researchers is as an indexing service, since the price for delivery is approximately $8.50 per article. The online tables of contents and bibliographic information for several thousand periodicals are extremely useful, though. Many researchers use it as a substitute for other indexes such as Social Sciences and Humanities Index, since it covers many of the same sources.

ERIC—the Educational Resources Information Center

ERIC is an educational database that consists of *Current Journals in Education* (CJIE) and *Resources in Education* (RIE). CJIE indexes professional journals in education and related fields; RIE indexes unpublished documents and reports. These texts are available on microfiche in most libraries. The CJIE index has been available for many years on CD-ROM. This set of resources is available without charge to anyone who has access to the Internet.

The ERIC system actually consists of sixteen subject-specific information databases called clearinghouses. ERIC is the largest education-oriented database in the entire world. Through ERIC, you can access journal articles, curriculum guides, and abstracts of many articles.

Encyclopedias and Other References

Although many standard references sources such as *Roget's Thesaurus* and *Webster's Dictionary* are available online, standard encyclopedias are still under copyright and thus can only be made available to schools that subscribe to their services. The *Encyclopaedia Britannica* (http://www.ebec.com) is found on many college Web sites, even on those with few other copyrighted databases. If your college does not subscribe, you can purchase an individual subscription. You can also sign up for a free trial subscription.

The Internet community has developed The Free Internet Encyclopedia to fill the void (http://www.eff.org). This is a wonderful example of the way people across the world collaborate to build information resources that are needed, and it fills a gap that traditional encyclopedias don't cover since its purpose is to provide access to information through the Internet. It is not, however, nearly as reliable as print analogues, since the entries that are added are not authenticated.

To find standard references such as dictionaries and style guides on the Web, use a search tool such as WebCrawler and search for the type of tool you want—dictionary, encyclopedia, etc. When you find items that you want to refer to readily, bookmark them. (See chapter 8 for suggestions on how to organize your bookmarks.) If you go to the Web site for this text (chapter 5, Web Links), you can click on any of the items below and then bookmark them when they appear on your screen.

SAMPLE REFERENCE COLLECTIONS

Reference Desk Collection
General Reference Resources via Gopher Jewels
On-Line Ready Reference (SOLINET)
Virtual Reference Desk (U of Calif-Irvine)
Nysernet Reference Desk

SAMPLE SOURCES IN REFERENCE COLLECTIONS

Roget's Thesaurus Search (from NIH)
Today's Foreign Currency Exchange Rates
U.S. Congressional Directory (1993)
U.S. Geographic Database (Search by ZIP Code or City Name)
U.S. Postal Service Abbreviations

U.S. Telephone Area Codes
U.S. ZIP Code Directory (from Brown Univ.)
Unit Conversion Tables
Acronym Dictionary Search (Australia)
Best Market Reports (UMich)
CIA World Factbook 1993 (Searchable) at NWOCA
CIA World Factbook 1994 (Searchable) at NWOCA
CIA World Factbook 1995 (CIA)
Currency Exchange Rates (UN)
Dictionary: American English Dictionary (Sonoma State)
Dictionary: German/English Dictionary (UToledo)
Dictionary: Swahili Dictionary Gopher (Yale)
Dictionary: Webster's Dictionary & Thesaurus (MemSt)
Elementary & Fundamental Particles of Matter
Geographic Name Server
Geologic Progression Timetable
International System of Units
Mathematical Values
Monetary Statistics
Periodic Table of the Elements (rev. 3/93)
World Telephone Area Code Directory

Newspapers

Even though some newspapers offer only subscription access, most newspapers are available for no fee on the Web. Some newspapers, including *The New York Times,* shown in figure 5.5, require you to go through a registration process the first time you use the online version. As you examine different newspapers, notice that some have incorporated new features to tap the potential of the Web. For example, *The New York Times* has an online forum that takes the print-based notion of Letters to the Editor to a new level of interactivity. A sample screen from the forum is shown in figure 5.6. Here are some newspaper sites you should explore as possible resources for your research:

Linkname: Steve's Online Newspapers
http://www.mediainfo.com:4900/ephome/npaper/nphtm/online.htm

This page includes almost every online newspaper in the world. It even includes a map which lets you get a list of newspapers by continent. The search engine allows you to locate newspapers.

Figure 5.5   *The New York Times* on the Web.

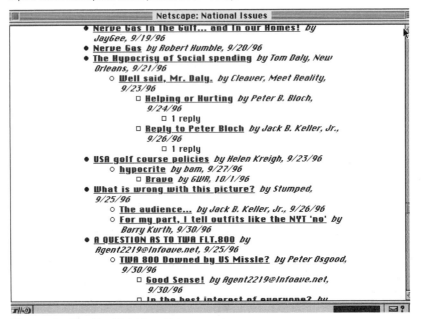

Figure 5.6   *The New York Times* Forums page.

Newspaper Association of America (NAA) Web Site
http://www.Infi.Net/Naa/Hot.Html

Features newspapers from around the country, including *The Atlanta Journal & Constitution, The Boston Globe, The Chicago Tribune, The Dallas Morning News, The New York Times,* and many small-town newspapers.

Reuters News Media
http://www.reuters.com

A service of Global News Network, Reuters is a well-organized Internet newspaper which focuses on the business community. The purpose is to "help you get to critical business information, when and where you need it." The Reuters database contains more than 2,100 periodicals, newspapers, trade journals, financial reports, news wires, and research documents. It also features world news coverage.

Government Publications

Government offices have moved to the Web quickly. Not only does being on the Web help them save on expenses, it also serves as a public relations tool. People are happier with an agency whose services and information they can access speedily. Some government sources you should explore are listed below. If you go to the Web site for this text, you can click on any of these items and then bookmark them when they appear on your screen.

Government Documents
gopher://wiretap.spies.com

Includes full-test of government acts. Also has NATO and White House press releases.

Mother Jones Interactive
http://www.mojones.com/mojo_interactive/mojo_interactive.html

This page is organized into issue-oriented areas, including such items as "Waging Peace" and "Improving Our Nation's Education." Includes complete text of *Mother Jones Magazine* and chat rooms where you can "talk" online about issues.

U.S. Bureau of the Census

http://www.census.gov/

Provides news releases, population information, and demographic data.

Thomas

http://thomas.loc.gov/

Offers the full text of bills from the 103d and 104th Congresses, searchable by bill number or keyword(s) or browsable by bill type. THOMAS also provides the full text of *The Congressional Record* for the 103d and 104th Congresses, searchable by keyword(s) or speaker or browsable by date and part.

Welcome to the White House

http://www.whitehouse.gov

Offers White House information such as daily press releases and briefings.

U.S. Government Today

gopher://wiretap.spies.com

Includes membership lists for House and Senate members, including their addresses and phone numbers.

United States Federal Web Locator

http://www.law.vill.edu/Fed-Agency/fedwebloc.html

A service provided by theVillanova Center for Information Law and Policy. You'll find information on almost any aspect of the federal government here, as it is intended to be a kind of one-stop shop for information about the federal government as well as a way of locating federal agencies.

Congressional Record, Government Printing Office, etc. (via Purdue University)

http://thorplus.lib.purdue.edu/gpo/

This is a searchable set of databases. You can select the item you want to search and search only the contents of that specific database or you can search the entire site. Categories included are:

Congressional Bills
Congressional Calendars
Congressional Directory
Congressional Documents
Congressional Record
Congressional Record Index
Congressional Reports
Economic Indicators
Economic Report of the President
Federal Register
General Accounting Office
Government Manual
History of Bills
Privacy Act Issuances
Public Laws
United States Code

FAMILIAR STARTING POINTS
FOR LIBRARY SOURCES
ON THE WEB

Libraries in virtual form have begun to appear on the Web. For example, the Internet Public Library (figure 5.7) is an ongoing project of library staff at the University of Michigan. If you choose to do your Internet surfing using a virtual library as a starting point, you may feel more comfortable than if you start exploring on your own. Library sites such as Inter-Links and the InfoSurf Library Gopher offer robust collections of information for researchers. Inter-Links uses traditional categories to group its collection of sources; it is this kind of collection that will help you make the transition from library searching to Web searching.

The Internet Public Library
http://aristotle.sils.umich.edu/

The Internet Public Library is a growing collection you'll want to visit, whether or not your campus offers a collection of reference tools on CD-ROM. The virtual library even includes an online reference librarian (in a pilot project).

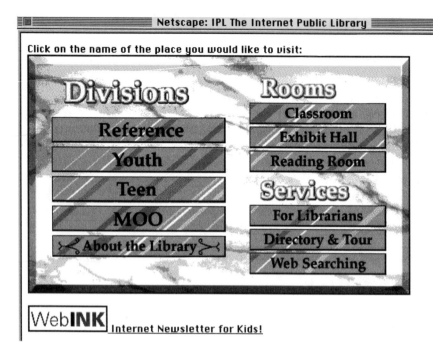

Figure 5.7   Internet Public Library.

InfoSurf Library Gopher

http://www.library.ucsb.edu

This gopher site from the University of California-Santa Barbara provides an excellent collection of links to library resources and to Web-based information. It includes such items as electronic journal listings, reference collections, library tutorials, and pointers to such sites as the Library of Congress, the Los Angeles Public Library, and the YaleInfo gopher.

Library Resources—Inter-Links

http://www.nova.edu/Inter-Links/start.html

Inter-Links was created by Rob Kabacoff, Ph.D., from the Center for Psychological Studies at Nova Southeastern University in Fort Lauderdale, Florida. Figure 5.8 shows one page from that collection.

Full Text
  * Books and Poetry
  * Journals and Magazines

Card Catalogs
  * Library Catalogs - Gopher
  * Library Catalogs - HYTELNET

Literature Searches
  * Search Book Titles - RLG
  * Search Journal Titles - UnCover

Other Resources
  * Florida Library Consortium
  * Library of Congress Web
  * Libraries with Web Interfaces
  * Libcat: Library Resource Guide

Figure 5.8   Some Inter-Links menu choices.

CONCLUSION

Many of the resources you will use in your research can be either located on the Web or accessed directly from the Web. Much information is in familiar genres—journals, newspapers, and government documents—that have been reformatted for the Web. Other resources are collections of information that didn't exist before the Internet and the Web (e.g., online museums, discussion forums, etc.).

Some of the books and journal articles that you locate in other libraries will not be available to you in your own library, but at least you'll have the advantage of knowing what's been written in your area of interest. As you begin searching, you'll find out just what sources suit your needs, which of those are available on the Web, and which require a trip to a nearby library. Don't avoid going to the library. Even students with access to online journals will need to use the library to locate books.

If you explore only a few of the resources described in this chapter you will no doubt recognize that libraries and librarians are emerging as supporters of Internet development. They are cooperating with one another and with Web enthusiasts everywhere to build a future virtual library that will be fully integrated into the World Wide Web.

END-OF-CHAPTER EXERCISES

1. What sources do you usually use in your research? Which of these sources are available on the Web?
2. Find the Web sites for several of the traditional library sources mentioned in this chapter. Bookmark any sources you think you might use for your own research.
3. Share bookmark collections with your classmates. Evaluate one another's collections. Revise your own collection until you have a set of sources that you could truly use for your college, career, and personal needs.

SUGGESTIONS FOR RESEARCH AND WRITING

A current collection of sources related to these topics can be found at the Web site for this book.

1. Some universities and colleges have more funds than others and can, therefore, provide students with a more comprehensive collection of copyrighted sources. Is this fair? Are students at community colleges, state colleges, and state universities being cheated? Take a stand on this issue after examining it in depth. Visit a range of libraries and determine how extensive their collections of proprietary databases are. Survey students at different universities to determine whether they use the resources available to them.
2. Do people really read newspapers, periodicals, and books online? Do a research project in which you examine reading habits in the information age. Find out if people print out portions of online texts. See if you can determine whether most online papers are accessed by search engines that ferret out articles and past search results rather than by people who want to read in a way similar to the way they read printed newspapers.
3. What similarities exist between the transition from oral to print cultures and the shift from a print-based society to an electronic age? Explore the who, what, where, and how of access to print sources. Propose the best ways for all people to have access to online sources. Is it at home? in libraries? in post offices?

CHAPTER 6

FINDING RESOURCES IN THE DISCIPLINES

Different fields of study value different kinds of research. If you are conducting scientific research or doing a paper for the natural sciences, you'll have different needs when you turn to the World Wide Web than will someone in the social sciences or humanities. As you become an experienced researcher, you'll discover ways to streamline the process of finding information. The more you learn about advanced search strategies, the better you'll be at finding what you need. But even the most experienced researchers make some of their best finds by accident, by just stumbling over valuable information. The suggestions that follow should help guarantee that you will stumble onto something valuable while you surf the net. After presenting some advanced search strategies that you should consider using if you are conducting specialized research, this chapter includes a brief overview of subject area sites on the Web and a list of key resources in various disciplines.

USING ADVANCED SEARCH STRATEGIES FOR RESEARCH IN THE DISCIPLINES

If you are trying to find specialized information on a topic, you should learn how to search in specialized areas of the Internet such as Gopher sites, WAIS databases, and FTP sites.

Gopher

As explained in chapter 2, Gopher is a program developed at the University of Minnesota that enables information to be stored easily without alteration (i.e., the markup language HTML must be used to ready docu-

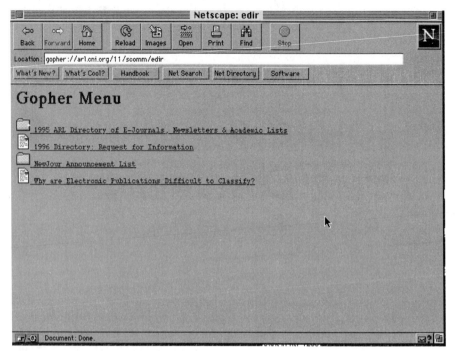

Figure 6.1   Gopher menu.

ments for the Web); as a result, many sites still use Gopher to store vast quantities of data. Project Gutenberg is an example of a site that uses Gopher software to organize its collection of books and other texts. You can access Gopher sites through your Web browser or by using a Gopher program (if one is available to you). Figure 6.1 shows an example of a Gopher menu. When you click on a Gopher site that you want to examine, your computer automatically opens a connection to that site. As you click on a new site, the computer closes the current connection and opens the next. Here are the basics of using a Gopher site from your Web browser:

1. Double-click on a folder to open the folder.
2. Double-click on a text file to display the text of the document.
3. Double-click on a Telnet icon to launch a Telnet session.
4. Double-click on a question mark to search within a database.
5. Double-click on a phone book icon to search within a phone book.

Even though most search engines include Gopher sites in their searches, many Gopher sites do not provide access to the texts of documents, thus Web searching will only pick up those sites in which the keywords appear in titles or directories. Many Gopher sites that you find have their own search tool (usually based on a program called Jughead) that enables you to search that individual site.

If you want to search multiple Gopher sites, you need to use a tool called Veronica. Veronica stands for Very Easy Rodent-Oriented Net-wide Index to Computerized Archives and, as you may have guessed, it was named after Veronica in the comic books—Archie's girlfriend. Most Gopher sites include Veronica as an option you can use.

There are many valuable resources available at Gopher sites. Here is a sample:

weather maps	wx.atmos.uiuc.edu
White House press releases	wiretap.spies.com
WELL archive	gopher.well.sf.ca.us
Supreme Court rulings	ashpool.micro.umn.edu
Electronic Frontier archive	gopher.eff.org

If you want to navigate a Gopher site using Gopher software rather than your Web browser, you can either use the software at your own site (if it is available) or Telnet to one of the following sites:

consultant.micro.umn.edu	log in as **gopher**
library.wustl.edu	No login required
panda.uiowa.edu	No login required

WAIS

Use WAIS (Wide Area Information Server) to look through material that has been indexed in special WAIS databases. Whereas most search tools scour the Web well, they examine only those pages that have been marked up using HTML. But some data on the Web is not directly in HTML code; it is, instead, buried in databases that have been organized using WAIS software.

With WAIS, you can search for information at many WAIS sites at once, since the WAIS search engine looks at WAIS databases on computers throughout the world (see box on WAIS sources organized by subject). WAIS indexes consist of all words in all documents. Unfortunately, you can't limit the search with Boolean operators. As a result, if you are searching for information on environmental pollution caused by acid rain, you'd have to search for pollution and manually sift through the results until you found those that have to do with acid rain. You can go to the following site and use the WAIS search program available for general use: gopher://gopher gw.micro.umn.edu:70/11/WAISes/Everything. This program allows you to search more than 600 different databases.

WAIS SOURCES ORGANIZED BY SUBJECT (FROM SOUTH-WESTERN LOUISIANA UNIVERSITY)

(DIR) [42]Veronica, Keyword Searches of Gopher Menus World-wide

(DIR) [43]WAIS-Based Information

(DIR) [44]WAIS sources organized by subject (from SLU)

(DIR) [45]WELL Gopher-space, an Electronic Magazine

(DIR) [46]Webster's Dictionary

(DIR) [47]Wieviel Uhr ist es in . . . ?

(DIR) [48]World Factbook 1992

FTP (and Archie)

Occasionally, you will see references to FTP (File Transfer Protocol) sites, locations for many interesting and useful resources (text files, graphics, etc.) that people have made available in directories of their computers. It takes time to format texts for the Web or to place them in Gopher menus. FTP is a way of getting useful information that hasn't been placed on Gopher or Web servers. Archie is a program that was developed to help you find FTP sites. It indexes FTP sites and lists the files available at each site. An Archie server is a special computer that has been set up to regularly check Internet sites to see if new FTP files have been added. If it locates new sites, it adds them to its ever-expanding database. If you have an Archie server on your own computer, use it. If not, you can access Archie at either of the following sites by telneting to that site. Remember to log in as archie (Login: archie).

o USA [NY]: telnet archie.ans.net

o USA [NJ]: telnet archie.rutgers.edu

Archie searches for files and directories that match the search criteria you enter. Try using the **what is** search feature. This command tells Archie to search an index of file descriptions. For example, if you are searching for information on affirmative action, you would type the following:

archie> **what is affirmative action**

If your research involves searching many Archie sites, you may want to get into the habit of sending the results of your search to your e-mail address. To do this, you type **mail emailaddress** and press <Enter>. If you want, you can even store your e-mail address by typing **set mailto emailaddress.**

If you want to examine a list of FTP sites themselves, type **list** and press <Enter>. You can then go to these sites and explore them on your own. (Type the URL for the site into your Web browser.) Here are some addresses of FTP archives:

Univ. of Minn. Menu of FTP Archives
gopher://gopher.tc.umn.edu/11/FTP%20S

Washington University Archive
file://wuarchive.wustl.edu/

University of Michigan MERIT Archives
gopher://gopher.archive.merit.edu:70/11.software-archives

http://www.bubl.bath.ac.uk/BUBL/Key.html

PRACTICE BOX

1. Work with a partner to explore various Gopher sites. What do you like about Gopher? Can you see any advantage to using Gopher-style organization rather than the hypertext organization of the Web?

2. Work with a partner and explore a WAIS database on a subject of interest to you. Evaluate the results of your search. Did you find useful information? Would you recommend using WAIS?

3. Archie is an extremely primitive search tool compared to the sophisticated Web browsers you learned to use earlier in this book. Is it worth the trouble? Try searching for your topic with a search tool such as one of those listed in chapter 2. Then search for the same topic using Archie. Compare the results of your search.

SUBJECT-AREA COLLECTIONS

To locate resources in your discipline, gain a basic familiarity with the many subject-area collections on the Web. Subject-area collections contain organized links about various topics or fields of study. These compendiums of information, in turn, contain pointers to specific-subject area data. The subject-area links and, in the case of the Clearinghouse, bibliographies of information, have been gathered by individuals or groups of people with interest and expertise in the topics.

You will be creating your own customized subject-area list as you develop a bibliography for your research project. Use existing subject-area lists either to start your research or to explore areas of interest at any point in the research process. Below you will find some of the key subject guides on the Internet. To find additional guides, use the search tools described in chapter 3 and search for "subject" or "subject guides." Also, check the very fine subject guide collections that librarians have put together. (Some of these lists are included in Librarian-Built Subject Guides at http://www.intac.com/~kgs/sublib.html.)

The BUBL Information Source

http://www.bubl.bath.ac.uk/BUBL/key.html

Maintained by subject-area specialists from different places, the BUBL Information Source (originally BUBL for **Bu**lletin **B**oard for **L**ibraries) provides a variety of information specifically for the academic and research communities. BUBL is based at the University of Strathclyde in Scotland. It offers many services, including a list of Internet current issues in an area called BUBL Updates. You will probably be most interested in the BUBL WWW Subject Tree—Arranged by Universal Decimal Classification:

0-Reference Works
003-Writing, Semiotics
008-Cultures and Civilizations
009-The Humanities
069-Museums
07-Journalism, Newspapers
14-Philosophy
15/159.9-Psychology
17-Ethics, Morals, Convention
20-Religion, Theology
30-Social Sciences
30-Sociology
31-Statistics
32-Political Science, Politics-Economics
34-Law and Legislation

343-Crime, Criminal Law and Criminology
347-Copyright, Intellectual Property
35-Public Administration, Government
36-Social Relief, Welfare, Insurance
362.65-Disability Issues
369.4-Community and Youth Studies
37-Education
38-Banks and Banking
396-Women and Society, Feminism
398-Custom, Folklore, Social Anthropology

5-Science
502.7-Nature and Wildlife
   Protection
51-Mathematics
518-Computing, Computer
   Science
52-Astronomy
53-Physics
54-Chemistry
55-Earth Sciences
55-Geology
551.46-Oceanography
551.5-Meteorology
551.588-Environmental Issues
56-Paleontology
57-Biology
571/572-Anthropology,
   Anthropobiology
575-Genetics
576.8-Microbiology
58-Botany
59-Zoology
62-Engineering

620.1-Engineering Material
621-Mechanical Engineering
621.3-Electronics
624-Civil Engineering
65-Management
654.1-Broadcasting
655.4/5-Publishing and Book-
   selling
657-Accounting
658-Business
658.8-Marketing
66-Chemical Engineering
663-Biotechnology
70-Arts, Artists, and the Arts
72-Architecture
77-Photography
78-Music
792-Theater
8-Linguistics, Language,
   Literature, Poetry
92-Biography
93-History
930. 26-Archaeology

The Clearinghouse for Subject-Oriented Internet Resource Guides
http://www.lib.umich.edu/chhome.html

This collection of guides to Internet resources was developed collaboratively by the University of Michigan's library and its School of Information and Library Science. The topical resource guides are prepared under faculty direction by experienced students and researchers. Each guide points to information about a specific topic that is available free of charge on the Internet. Most of the guides are about twenty pages long. They include a variety of Internet resources, including Gopher sites, WAIS databases, and mailing lists. Each guide includes the name and address of the author(s), along with a brief biography that indicates the author's expertise, which may help you check the validity of a source. The goal of the project is to provide a comprehensive index to everything on the Internet. The home page in figure 6.2 shows some of the choices available. The Clearinghouse pages can be browsed by following links or can be searched either in their entirety or by individual sections.

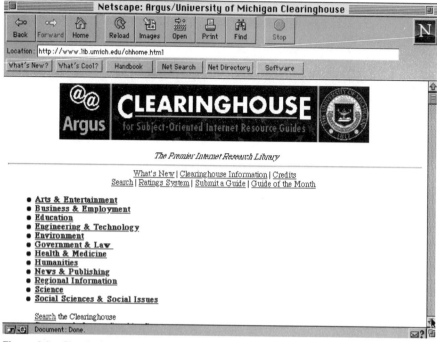

Figure 6.2   Clearinghouse home page.

The World Wide Web Virtual Library

http://www.w3.org/hypertext/DataSources/bySubject/Overview.html

The World Wide Web Virtual Library is a distributed subject catalog that can be viewed in various ways, through an alphabetical list, category subtrees, service types, or a Library of Congress organizational structure. To find a collection of information on a topic of interest to you, select the overall category, such as "technology," then select appropriate subcategories.

People with expertise in a given subject administer individual areas of the Virtual Library. You are encouraged to mail specific site information to the list maintainers so that they can keep updating it. Also, if you want to administer a subject area that has not been indexed, the developers of the WWW Virtual Library would like to hear from you. The subject headings in their database include:

Agriculture
Auxiliary Sciences of History
Bibliography. Library Science

Communications and Telecommunications
Education
Fine Arts
General Works
Geography. Anthropology. Recreation
History: America
History: General and Old World
Language and Literature
Law
Medicine
Military and Naval Science
Music and Books on Music
Philosophy. Psychology. Religion
Political Science
Science
Social Sciences
Technology

There are no search tools that allow you to search these pages independently, but the information in this catalog can be searched through the CUIW3 catalog (http://cuiwww.unige.ch/w3catalog) where you'll find other information in addition to that from the Virtual Library. If you look for the Virtual Library icon (an open book) you'll be able to identify the items on your list that are from the Virtual Library.

Gopher Jewels
http://galaxy.einet.net/GJ/

Gopher Jewels has a Web address, since it has been incorporated into Tradeware Galaxy, a commercial site with other services. The Gopher-based version of Gopher Jewels, created by David Riggins, is available through the University of Southern California-USCgopher.

Each subject area includes a fully searchable index. Here is a partial list of subjects:

000 - Generalities
100 - Philosophy
200 - Religion
300 - Social Science
333 - Environmental Issues
400 - Languages

500 - Natural Science
600 - Applied Science and Technology
700 - Arts and Recreation
800 - Literature
900 - Geography and History

RESEARCHING THE DISCIPLINES

If you know the specific subject area you want to explore, you can search for that subject using the Internet search tools described in chapter 3 or using one of the specific references provided in the following sections, which refer to home page sites in key areas across the curriculum. All of these were located using the subject-area catalogs referred to in this chapter.

Humanities

Humanities scholars focus on texts. What most college students think of as a research paper is really the humanities' version of a research paper, for it contains what has been called "library research." Humanities researchers develop their insights by reading and reviewing text-based research by other scholars. Humanities researchers typically use the style guide *MLA Handbook for Writers of Research Papers* (Modern Language Association of America, 1995). Often in humanities papers, you are asked to support your own opinion. Before you rush to sources on either the Internet or in the library, take time to read the primary texts you have been assigned—in literature, philosophy, etc. Your paper should support *your* opinion. The sources you consult may help you develop your opinion, but you should gain confidence in establishing your own point of view and then finding sources that support your angle on a topic. Here is a sample of the kinds of discipline-specific resources in the humanities that can be located through subject guides:

Carnegie Mellon English Server
http:english-www.hss.cmu.edu

Literary Resources On The Net
http://www.english.upenn.edu/~jlynch/Lit/

Literature Resources
http://nimrod.mit.edu/depts/humanities/lit/literature.html

Literature Webliography
http://www.lib.lsu.edu/hum/lit.html

English & Humanities Sites
http://odin.english.udel.edu/humanities/humanities.html

Literary Resources On The Net
http://www.english.upenn.edu/~jlynch/Lit/

Center for Electronic Texts in the Humanities (Princeton/Rutgers)
http://www.princeton.edu/~mccarty/humanist/

Voice of the Shuttle
http://humanitas.ucsb.edu/

The Perseus Project (hypertext Classics project)
http://www.perseus.tufts.edu

ARTS online Santa Cruz—Cool Links To Arts-Related Sites Of Interest
http://members.gnn.com/cuda/art/links.htm

CURRENT (Arts Wire)
http://www.artswire.org/Artswire/www/current.html

FineartForum Online Art Resources: Art Museums and Art History
http://www.msstate.edu/Fineart_Online/art-resources/museums.html

Philosophy at Large
http://www.liv.ac.uk/~srlclark/philos.html

Philosophy
http://www.phil.gu.se/Philosophy.html

Research Institute for the Humanities - Philosophy
http://www.arts.cuhk.hk/Philo.html

Index to Philosophy Resources on the Web
http://www.freenet.calgary.ab.ca/~kyasench/philosophyindex.html
(Score 56, Size

Philosophy
http://www.physics.wisc.edu/~shalizi/hyper-weird/philosophy.html

H-Net (Humanities Online Home Page)
http://h-net.2.msu.edu/lists/lists.cgi

Social Sciences

Social scientists examine social issues. They recognize that the results of their work are relative, since they are dealing with people, not chemical or scientific data. Nonetheless, they value controlled investigation and use a variety of research techniques including surveys, interviews, focus groups, and participant observation studies. (Zimmerman and Rodrigues, 1992). Since social scientists use survey research, they are likely to use areas on the Web that post data sets such as that used for the Lou Harris polls. Social scientists follow style guides such as *Publication Manual of the American Psychological Association* (American Psychological Association, 1994) and *The Chicago Manual of Style* (University of Chicago Press, 1993). Research papers in the social sciences often include headings and subheadings. Formal papers follow standard headings and subheadings: Abstract, Introduction, Methods, Results and Discussion, and Conclusion.

Coombs Collection
http://coombs.anu.edu.au/WWWVL-SocSci.html

Social Sciences—BUBL
http://www.bubl.bath.ac.uk/BUBL/Social_Sciences.html

in Motion (online multicultural magazine)
http://www.inmotionmagazine.com/

Voice of the Shuttle: History Page
http://humanitas.ucsb.edu/shuttle/history.html

European Borders: History Of Space/Space Of History
http://www.ctheory.com/a-european_borders.html

History Computerization Project
http://www.directnet.com/history/

American Studies Web: Historical Essays and Archival Resources
http://pantheon.cis.yale.edu/~davidp/archives.html

Local History Web Resources
http://www.spcc.com/ihsw/lhsresor.htm

Index of Resources for History
http://www.ukans.edu/history/

American and British History Resources on the Internet
http://info.rutgers.edu/rulib/artshum/amhist.html

Other History Links
http://ocaxpl.cc.oberlin.edu/~history/HistoryLinks.html

History Internet Resources
http://blair.library.rhodes.edu/histhtmls/histnet.html

Larry Schankman's Infoguide
http://www.clark.net/pub/lschank/

This guide includes the following categories:

International & Area Studies
Just Politics
Legislation and Regulations
State and Local Government
Voting and Elections

Government Information
http://info.umd.edu:901:11/info/Government/US

Infomine (See figure 6.3)
http://nln.com

Natural Sciences and Mathematics

Researchers in the natural sciences use experimental research methods to look for answers to their research questions. They use both direct experimentation and observation as their primary research techniques whether they work in the laboratory or in the field (Zimmerman and Rodrigues, 1992). For example, if researchers are trying to detect the radiation level in drinking water, they will perform lab experiments designed to isolate the presence of radioactive particles. If they are attempting to determine why wolves left Yellowstone, they are likely to

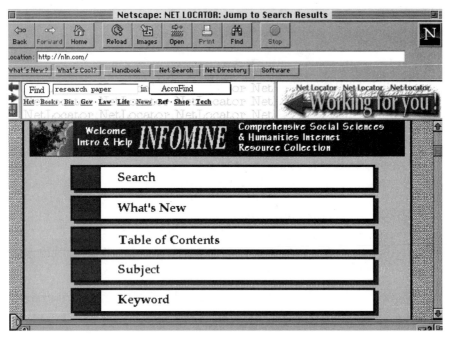

Figure 6.3   Infomine home page.

use observational methods, such as tracking wolves and tabulating their whereabouts.

Scientists' research questions usually have a prominent role in the beginning of a research report. The format for research reports is much like that followed by social scientists: Abstract, Introduction, Methods, Results and Discussion, Conclusions, and Summary. Scientists use the Web to share research results and to share data. Scientists and mathematicians use either the CBE style guide or the APA style guide.

WWW sites for biologists
http://www.abc.hu/biosites.html

Biology (Science)
http://doradus.einet.net/galaxy/Science/Biology.html

BUBL WWW Subject Tree - Biology
http://www.bubl.bath.ac.uk/BUBL/Biology.html

The World-Wide Web Virtual Library: Chemistry
http://pluto.njcc.com/~bpapp/chempoin.html

Chemistry Information on the Internet
http://hackberry.chem.niu.edu/cheminf.html

Math Gopher
gopher://riceinfo.rice.edu/70/11/Subject/Math

Physics Gopher
gopher://riceinfo.rice.edu/70/11/Subject/Physics

Penn State's Math Guide
http://www.math.psu.edu/OtherMath.html

WWW Virtual Library Math Guide
http://euclid.math.fsu.edu/Science/math.html

EInet Math Guide
http://galaxy.einet.net/galaxy/Science/Mathematics.html

Business

Research in Business varies with the field. Some fields of study follow the same documentation guidelines for research in Social Sciences. Other Business areas, in particular those related to statistical analysis, follow guidelines used by mathematics.

The Internet has many valuable business areas. There are discussion lists, file archives, web sites, and software collections available. One problem in using business resources on the Internet is that they change frequently. MIT keeps an updated reference service at http://tns-www.lcs.mit.edu/commerce.html. This listing provides users with the location of new resources.

BUBL WWW Subject Tree - Business
http://www.bubl.bath.ac.uk/BUBL/Business.html

Business
http://www.bubl.bath.ac.uk/BUBL/Business.html

Management
http://www.bubl.bath.ac.uk/BUBL/Management.html

Economics
http://www.bubl.bath.ac.uk/BUBl/Economics.html

Catalog of Federal Domestic Assistance
Gopher://marvel.loc.gov

The General Accounting Office
gopher://wiretap.spies.com

Business and Economics Web Server (Nijenrode)
http://www.nijenrode.nl/nbr/

Business Journals
http://www.businessjournals.com/

Business Process Re-engineering & Management Journal
http://www.mcb.co.uk/liblink/bprmj/jourhome.htm

CNN Financial News
http://cnnfn.com/

Dow Jones Directory
http://www.dowjones.com/

Institute for Business and Professional Ethics
http://www.depaul.edu/ethics/

Garbo (International Information)
gopher://garbo.uwasa.fiport 70

Latin American Information
gopher://info.lanic.utexas.edu 70

Canadian Information
gopher://talon.staatcan.ca

Small Business Information
http://incorporate.com/tcc/home.html

Education

Educators from the kindergarten level to universities have been actively developing sites for research and teaching.[1] Teachers of grades K

---

[1] For a good guide to resources about education, see Jill H. Ellsworth, *Education on the Internet: A Hands-on Book of Ideas, Resources, Projects, and Advice* (SAMS Publishing, 1995).

through 12 use the Internet to locate lesson plans, to collaborate with other classroom teachers, and to create and advertise Web projects of their own. College and university students and professors use Web sites for research and for display of information about their programs. The sites listed here focus primarily on K–12 education and are most useful for education majors or teachers. Educators follow either MLA or APA style guides, depending on their subject area specialty.

BUBL WWW Subject Tree - Education
http://www.bubl.bath.ac.uk/BUBL/Education.html

The Commonwealth of Learning
http://www.col.org/c10695.html

Jonathan Ross's Educational Hot Links
http://www.ucalgary.ca/~jross/Links.html

Jason Merry's Distance Education Directory
http://is.dal.ca/~jmerry/dist.htm

General Education Resources
http://www.teleport.com/~vincer/general.html

Math Forum Internet Collection - edlessons (Outline)
http://forum.swarthmore.edu/~steve/steve/edlessons.html

Ask Eric Virtual Library
http://ericir.syr.edu/Virtual/

Engineering

Engineering majors often have little room in the curriculum for writing courses, but they do considerable writing on the job. Technical writing areas on the Internet may be useful for you to explore if you are majoring in an engineering field. Background information for many engineering reports can be located on the Internet. Here are some samples of the kinds of information you can find:

Manufacturing Engineering Resources
http://marg.ntu.ac.uk/resources.html

EELS - Engineering Electronic Library
http://www.ub2.lu.se/eel/eelhome.html

The Scholes Library Engineering & Science Page
http://scholes.alfred.edu/EandS.html

Manufacturing Engineering Resources
http://marg.ntu.ac.uk/resources.html

The World-Wide Web Virtual Library: Engineering
http://arioch.gsfc.nasa.gov/wwwvl/engineering.html

Links to Engineering and IT related Services
http://www.iee.org.uk/Misc/otherwww.htm

Engineering Specific
http://www.iee.org.uk/Misc/otherwww.htm#engindex

CONCLUSION

This chapter has given you an overview of how to use subject collections to locate sources in your discipline. As new search tools and new subject categories are developed, it will be easier for you to keep track of sites in your field. To keep up with resources in your discipline, isolate some key sources and check them frequently. Set up your own bookmark list for discipline-based sources so that you can add new sites as you find them.

The next chapter describes e-mail, mailing lists, and newsgroups, three additional tools for researchers in the disciplines who want to keep up with new developments in their fields. By taking part in electronic discussions with people around the world who are interested in a specific topic, you will develop a sophisticated sense of the range of Internet sources available to you.

END-OF-CHAPTER EXERCISES

1. What are the best resources in your field? Working with others in your class or workgroup, collaborate on a collection of Internet sites. Write a brief annotation of each site, indicating its value. Post your collection to the Web site for this book.

2. Find an area of the Internet that relates to your major field. See if you can determine how that site was developed. Try to find out who was involved in collecting the information, who did the hypertext markup, and who funded the project. After you have determined how the site was developed, see if you can determine why the site was developed. What kind of information did the developers hope to share with others? Do you think that the site is being used as the developers hoped it would be used?

3. Share research papers with your colleagues or peers across the country. Post your research paper to the Web page for your class and add a link from the Web site for this book.

SUGGESTIONS FOR RESEARCH AND WRITING

A current collection of sources related to these topics can be found at the Web site for this book.

1. Develop a multimedia research project, one that uses audio and video resources to supplement text-based information. For example, if you are exploring scientific issues, include a link to a Web area that provides images of the scientific concept you are examining. If you are doing a history project, link to a site that includes sound recordings of events you are investigating. You will need to learn how to use HTML markup language for this project. You will not, however, need to post your project on the Web for all to see unless you want to.

2. Consider collaborating with one of the many K–12 schools on the Web for a research project. Some elementary schools might be interested in partnering with your class. You might, for example, do a research project that answers questions students want to know. Or you might help students with their research and write a research paper that explores and examines what K–12 students are doing with the Internet.

CHAPTER 7

E-MAIL, MAILING LISTS, AND NEWSGROUPS AS RESEARCH TOOLS

E-mail (electronic mail), mailing lists, and UseNet newsgroups (discussion groups on a wide variety of topics and issues) can all be used as research tools. E-mail allows you to write messages to people throughout the world who are specialists on your subject; mailing lists help researchers and specialists on specific topics share ideas quickly; and UseNet, which distributes newsgroups and resembles a bulletin board in format, includes groups of people, often experts on their topics, who post messages called articles to topical areas that can be searched for later retrieval.

Most Web browsers are all-purpose tools. That is, you can not only navigate from site to site on the Internet with these browsers, you can also read UseNet newsgroups directly from them. Recent browsers also integrate e-mail into their array of offerings. An advantage to using mail from within a browser is that you can attach pages you find on the Web in your messages and share them with friends or fellow researchers. You can also paste URLs into your messages and make it possible for recipients to visit Web sites that you refer to in your message. A disadvantage of using e-mail from within a browser is that the e-mail software may be inferior to standard e-mail software.

As you read each section that follows, explore the possibilities at your local site. Examine the features of your browser. If the browser used at your site does not integrate e-mail and newsgroups, you might want to find out if you can install a different browser on your own computer.

E-MAIL

When you write an e-mail message, your message travels across the Internet to your party's computer mailbox. If the person to whom you are writing checks his or her mail regularly, you may get a speedy response. E-mail from one part of the country can arrive at another within seconds.

If you use e-mail effectively, you can gather up-to-the-moment information about your topic from experts whose e-mail addresses you have available to you. It's not easy to just plunge in and become an effective e-mail user, however. You need to take your time. If you are a novice to e-mail use, you need to learn the correct conventions of addressing and composing e-mail messages. When you are writing to an expert on the topic, be polite, yet scholarly. Show your reader that you care about the topic and that you have done some preliminary reading before writing a message of inquiry. Also, show the reader that you respect his or her time by keeping your query short and direct. Try to end your message with a clear indication of what you want the reader to do as a result of your message.

Using E-mail for Data
Gathering: Questions to Ask

Whether you use e-mail for personal communication or for research, you should take time to learn the conventions of e-mail use. For each research project, answer these questions:

- Is e-mail the appropriate genre to use for your research inquiries? Would a letter be more appropriate?
- How can you find e-mail addresses of specialists on your topic? (Consider joining a mailing list on the topic. After reading its messages for several days, you'll begin to notice that respondents often defer to several people—the specialists on that list.)
- When is it more important to call or visit an expert rather than to send an e-mail note?

E-mail programs usually allow you to create folders for different topics. If your e-mail program has this capability, learn how to use it. Organizing your e-mail in folders according to topic can help you find messages you want to incorporate into your research papers or reports. (See chapter 8 for a discussion of ways to organize notes for research.)

The Etiquette of E-mail: Netiquette

You can gather much information for your research projects by using e-mail effectively. But to get good results, you should learn about the etiquette of e-mail use, "netiquette." Since e-mail is a new form of writing, conventions for using e-mail effectively are still emerging. As with conventions for other genres of written communication, e-mail conventions vary from one context to another.

There are general conventions that will vary with the purpose and the audience of your message. If you are sending e-mail to a casual friend, you may be able to ignore these conventions. If you are attempting to get information from someone you do not know, it is best to follow these guidelines, remembering that they are only guidelines, not absolute rules:

- Keep messages to a page in length.
- Try to write about only one topic in each e-mail message. It's difficult for readers to remember what you said if you cover more than one topic.
- Don't type in all capital letters. Readability research has shown that readers can process text that contains both upper- and lowercase letters more easily than they can process all uppercase text.
- Vary your e-mail style to match your audience. E-mail is informal, but if you are writing to a superior or to an expert in your field, you need to be careful not to offend him or her. When you write to someone you don't know, you may need to remove some clever signature file that you typically include on your casual e-mail.
- Don't be overly concerned about error. Errors are tolerated on e-mail for several reasons: (1) people make mistakes when they try to write as fast as they are thinking (and e-mail is more like talking than like writing); (2) many people do not have spell-checkers on their e-mail systems; and (3) many systems don't adjust line length when changes are made, so people don't take the time to correct errors.
- When replying to e-mail, don't copy the entire message into your response. Instead, either copy the portion of the message to which you are responding or refresh your reader's memory by referring to the topic of his or her message.

Creating and Sending E-mail Messages to Request Information

To create an e-mail message, follow the directions for the e-mail package you use. Typically, you start an e-mail package by clicking on a "start" icon or by typing a command such as "mail." Then you fill out the header area—the **to, from,** and **subject** sections. Next, you write the message in the area of the e-mail program that is designed for the text of your message. Finally, you need to press whatever keys are required to **send** mail. If the e-mail system you are using doesn't automatically save a copy of the message you have sent, you may want to send a copy of the message to yourself. One way of doing this is to fill in the **cc:** area of the message with your own e-mail address and thus forward a copy of the message to yourself.

You should understand the different components of an e-mail address so that you can understand what makes e-mail work. E-mail addresses are usually in the form of **user@host.domain.** The **user** is the name of the recipient's mail account, or the names of a distribution list that in turn sends mail to many users. **Host.domain** is the full name of the host (computer) on which the user has a mail account.

Examples of Internet addresses are:

scarrie@meol.mass.edu

djones@aol.com

The address must be filled out correctly. It contains the information that sends the message to its proper location. Here is a sample e-mail message:

```
Date:     11/16/95
From:     scarrie@pigseye.kennesaw.edu
To:       rmunroe@washington.edu
CC:       [optional]
Subject:  software
- - - - - - - - - - - - - - - - - - - - - - - - - - - - - - - - - - - - -
[message area—where you either type your message or insert text
that you have composed with a word processor]
- - - - - - - - - - - - - - - - - - - - - - - - - - - - - - - - - - - - -
```

When the recipient of this message logs in to his or her computer, the message will look something like this:

```
Received:   from pigseye (scarrie) by pine (rmunroe)
Id 0521; (Mail R2.5) Thu, 16 Nov 95 12:42:33 EST
Received:   by pine(Mailer R2. 08 PTF008) id 5496;
Thu, 16 Nov 95 12:19:10 EST
Subject:   Re:literary response
References:<scarrie>.921111141141@pigseye.kennesaw.ed
Message-ID: <rmunroe.921121218170pigseye.kennesaw.edu
From:  scarrie@pigseye.kennesaw.edu (Sarah Carrie)
```

To: rmunroe@washington.edu (Rick Munroe)
Date: Fri, 16 Nov 95 12:18:17 EST

I am a student in an English Education class at Kennesaw State College. I have read several books on literary response theories, but have not had a chance to find out how response theory is used in high school classrooms. If you have the time, I'd appreciate hearing about whether you use literary response techniques and what techniques you use.

Sarah Carrie

Finding People on E-mail

It's still not easy to find someone's e-mail address on the Internet, but there are some ways you can try. *Who's Where* (www.whowhere.com) is a White Pages service that helps you identify people whose educational institutions or companies have registered their sites. When you initiate a search, you are asked to provide the name of the institution as well as the name of the person you are trying to locate. To make it easy for you to locate people and businesses, Netscape 3.0 has added a button on its menu bar called Net Find. Clicking "Net Find" brings you to a list of search programs designed to locate Internet users. Another good way to find someone's e-mail address is to check the web site for his or her college or university. Many institutions include a directory of both faculty and students on their home page.

If you are trying to find the e-mail address of an expert on your topic, one way is to subscribe to a mailing list related to your topic and read messages that list participants send to one another. When you get a sense of which participants appear to have special expertise on a given topic, you can compose an e-mail question just to that person instead of posing the question to the entire list.

MAILING LISTS

What is a mailing list? It is a system for sending e-mail to a group of people who are interested in a common topic. A computer called a list server distributes mail sent to people who have joined the mailing list. (LISTSERV by Eric Thomas and LISTPROC by Anastasio Kotsikonas are two of the most popular mailing list programs.) Mailing lists are more or less focused discussions on topics ranging from television shows to political issues to business practices to almost anything imaginable. Messages sent to the list are received by all subscribers. This section will show you how to subscribe to a list; it will also help you understand some subtleties of mailing lists so that you do not embarrass yourself unnecessarily when you write your first messages.

Subscribing to a Mailing List

To subscribe to a list, send a simple request to an address in the form list-request@hostname:

```
To:  listserv@.ncte.org
subscribe <listname> <first name last name>
```

For example:

```
subscribe ncte-talk Dawn Rodrigues
```

Do not put anything into the subject area of the message, and do not include your e-mail address. Your address is automatically included in the header of every e-mail message you send.

The above message sends a message to the computer that maintains the list rather than to every recipient on the mailing list. The computer adds you to the list of subscribers. In less than a day, you should receive a return message such as the following from the server:

```
You have been successfully added to the list NCTE-Talk
```

You will also be sent information telling you how to quit the list and telling you what other commands you can use. Since commands for exiting lists sometimes vary, you need this information so that you can quit when your research project ends. Store messages explaining specialized commands for your mailing lists in a separate folder on your computer.

Following is a list of possible LISTSERV commands you can use. Other listserver software uses similar commands.

Info	Get detailed information files
List	Get a description of all lists
SUBscribe	Subscribe to a list listname <full_name>
SIGNOFF listname	Signoff from a list
REView	Review the list of subscribers
STatslistname	Review list statistics
Query	Query personal distribution options list name
SET listname	Set personal distribution options <options>
INDex filelist_name	Obtain a list of LISTSERV files
GET filename	Obtain a file from LISTSERV filetype
REGister	Tell LISTSERV about your name full_name OFF

Mailing List Basics

When you send a message to a mailing list, you are really sending it to the computer that handles the list. If you have questions, you need to write to the owner of the list. When you reply to a message on a mailing list, you can either reply to the author of the message or to everyone subscribing to the list.

Get familiar with the peculiarities of the lists to which you subscribe. Find out whether your list is a moderated list or an unmoderated list. With a moderated list, the list owner reads each message before it is posted; in some cases, that person may even introduce or summarize the message. With unmoderated lists, every message submitted is posted. Also learn about how your mail program handles list messages. In most mail programs, pressing **Reply** sends your message not to the author of the message, but to the entire list. Even experienced mailing list members make mistakes (accidentally posting messages to the entire list). But as a newcomer, you certainly don't want to draw attention to your mistakes. So be especially careful the first few times you send messages to a list.

It is a good idea to sign your name at the end of your e-mail message since not all e-mail programs will show readers your full name. If you can, set up a signature file in your e-mail program; this file will automatically insert your name and any other information you choose, such as your school affiliation and your phone number.

Mailing lists are intended to be informative and useful to participants. Each message should, ideally, either comment on a previous message or start a new "thread." If you are new to a list, you may want to introduce yourself before plunging in with a new topic or area of interest. Also, as a rule, do not send a message to a list until you have subscribed to the list for at least a week. By reading what others write, you can get a sense of the kinds of questions appropriate for the particular list.

PRACTICE BOX

1. If possible, practice using a mailing list by creating one for your class or your workgroup. In your first message, post your name and your research interests. (Ask the computer center operators at your school if they will create mailing lists for student groups.) In subsequent messages, respond to one another. Share ideas, discuss issues, probe your topics. This kind of informal discussion with people you know can be useful for topic exploration. It can also give you practice staying with a topic thread and learning how to introduce a new thread. When you are continuing a discussion, say something like: "I want to add a point to the discussion on [spe-

cific aspect of topic]" to help your readers. If your readers want, they can easily delete the message. When you want to change the topic of discussion, say something like, "I'd like to switch to a different topic for a minute."

2. Experiment with different ways of running a discussion. Select someone to moderate a list for several weeks. Do you prefer a moderated or an unmoderated list?

Using Mailing Lists for Research

Each mailing list group is a culture of its own, with conventions that have evolved gradually over time. Discussions on e-mail, mailing lists, and UseNet are not always as open as they appear to be. For example, on a list called Techwri-L—a list for technical writers—some participants tried to make the list more provocative and less purely technical. They were told to stop. A message titled "Off-Topic Issues on Techwri-L" made it clear that certain topics were acceptable and others were not.

If you get involved in a discussion, you should realize that as a newcomer you should not try to change the culture of the group. You can observe, however, how other members of the list disagree with one another and notice the consequences. If you do become an established member of a given list, don't let yourself be completely muzzled by the conventions. Instead, find ways to say what you want to say. Don't assume that the way people behave on one list is automatically acceptable on another. For example, some list owners (the individuals who set up the lists) do not want people to "flame" or taunt one another; on other lists, however, contributors are encouraged to push the limits of a given topic. There are some common guidelines you can follow:

1. Complete the **subject** area of your message carefully so that subscribers to a list can delete any messages related to topics they choose not to read.

2. If you are "flamed" for asking a silly question, don't be too upset. Remember, these people may all know each other and may have discussed your topic many times.

3. Contribute generously to the Web if you take from it. If you are doing research on Web browsers, for example, you might ask, "What is your favorite browser? What characteristics do you like about it?" Then offer to send your results to the list so that you help those who have helped you.

Finding Mailing Lists on Your Topic:

For a complete list of Internet mailing lists on your topic, send a message to the following address:

listserv@vm1.nodak.edu

In your message, include the following text:

```
list global/[your topic]
e.g., list global/library
```

When you determine which mailing lists interest you, subscribe to several lists. Your subscription information should include directions on accessing the archives for that list.

Another way to get a good directory of mailing lists is to access Diane Kovacs's *Guide to Mailing Lists* (ftp://ksuvxa.kent.edu in the library/subdirectory). This guide is designed to help researchers find mailing lists in their discipline. Diane Kovacs of Kent State University maintains a comprehensive list of academic LISTSERV groups, categorized by discipline. This list is available through the University of Michigan Clearinghouse referred to in chapter 6. These files can be retrieved through e-mail by sending a message to listserv@kentvm.kent.edu with the message:

```
get acadlist file4
```

Even if you don't plan to get involved in the discussion list, pay attention to what others do and say. The insights you gain by observing conventions on one list will help cut your learning time in the future. As a beginner to Internet research, you need to realize that you are in a strange land with conventions that you may never have seen before. Take time to get to know the list you are thinking about sending a message to. Don't write (as did one of my students): "I'm interested in creative drama. I need information for a paper." You're likely to get a response such as the one she got: "Have you heard of libraries? There are lots of books on that subject." Instead, say something like, "I'm interested in creative drama. I've read several books on the topic and noticed that the authors talk about successful practices, not about difficulties in using the technique. Have you had any problems getting students to cooperate?"

USENET NEWSGROUPS
FOR RESEARCH

In contrast to a mailing list, a newsgroup is a "bulletin board" where individual messages are posted. Instead of messages coming directly to your mailbox, news messages go directly to the computer that hosts the news software. To read news messages, you have to go to the newsgroup to find out what's been posted. Some people prefer mailing lists; others prefer newsgroups. The advantage of newsgroups is that the messages are not stored on your computer. The disadvantage is that the messages do not stay on the newsgroup bulletin board indefinitely. If you think that you want to use a message in your research paper, you should save it to a file as soon as possible.

Computer users in the early eighties who used the net coined the term UseNet after they put the news system together. UseNet is made up of many categories or newsgroups.

Newsgroups are considered to be distributed systems. Messages don't all reside on a central computer. Rather, messages from different people are transferred to whatever computer manages a given topic.

You can locate information for research projects by reading UseNet newsgroup messages devoted to your topic. Messages sent to newsgroups sound the same as those posted to mailing lists, for their purpose is similar and some of them coexist as mailing lists.

To access newsgroups, you may be able to use your Web browser. If your Web browser does not support news access, you can access UseNet sites directly from the Web by accessing the "UseNet info center launch pad" (http://sunsite.unc.edu/usenet-i/home.html). There you'll find the following choices:

Browse the UseNet Groups
Search for a UseNet Group
UseNet FAQs
Search UseNet News (DejaNews)
Other UseNet Indexes/Services

A filtering service called NetNews Filter Service (http://woodstock. stanford.edu:2000/) is available to help you find information you need. Established at Stanford University, the purpose of this service is to help people sift through the many newsgroups available and find the information that they need for their research. Stanford's NetNews Filter Service works like this: You send an e-mail note to the service. In your note you include the keywords you want the service to search. The next day, you get the results of your search in an e-mail message. Periodically, the service updates you on new information found on your topic.

Students in Michael Day's technical writing class at the South Dakota School of Mines and Technology are asked to try to find information for their class projects by writing to experts on their topics. Day encourages students to request information, to answer questions of others on the newsgroup or list, or to gather facts and opinions using a survey or questionnaire. Day explains one successful request:

> One student was writing a proposal on upgrading our school's Auto-Cad software and needed information about what version of the software other schools used. . . . He sent in his question to the AutoCad discussion list and received 6 responses over the next few days.
>
> Michael Day, "Writing in the Matrix: Students Tapping the Living Database on the Computer Network" (in Galin and Latchaw, NCTE, 1996).

Cybersociety: Computer-Mediated Communication and Community (ed., Steven G. Jones, Thousand Oaks, CA: Sage, 1995) includes several chapters about research into UseNet groups. The authors argue that ways of behaving in a UseNet group are self-regulated by the members. In other words, participants tend to correct their own conduct until it fits the norms of the group. Another chapter explores the topic of identity on UseNet groups and finds that even when people have the option of being anonymous, they prefer using their real names.

Newsgroup availability varies from site to site. The local computer administrator can decide which newsgroups to maintain at a given location. Newsgroups are arranged in hierarchical (tree) fashion. Each "root" of the tree is devoted to a given aspect of the general topic. Here are some of the major roots for newsgroups:

alt	Alternative newsgroups; anything and everything goes; anarchy
bionet	Biology-related newsgroups
biz	Business and related topics
comp	Computer topics including: hardware, software, operating systems, and network protocols
gnu	News covering software from the Free Software Foundation
ieee	Institute of Electrical and Electronics Engineers newsgroups (engineering topics)
k12	For students in grades K–12, and discussion of education
misc	Miscellaneous newsgroups that do not fit into other categories; multiple topics

news	Newsgroups about news, news network
rec	Recreation-related newsgroups
sci	Science newsgroups: research or applications of established sciences
soc	Sociology and socializing issues related to world cultures
talk	Newsgroups for the discussion on a specific topic; long debates

OTHER RESEARCH TOOLS

After you become familiar with Web discussion tools such as e-mail, mailing lists, and newsgroups, consider exploring other Internet programs such as forums, IRCs, and MOOs. As the Web develops, new tools emerge. You should explore new kinds of communication tools that you read about.

Bruce Dobler and Harry Bloomberg, professors at the University of Pittsburgh, feel strongly that research projects that ignore the Internet are not acceptable pieces of work. They are particularly excited about the promise of UseNet, listserver discussion groups, and MOOs (explained later in this chapter) for research.

> Active on-line discussion in MOOs and various real-time chat rooms create an interactive research space. Documents that would have remained unpublished or published to very limited audiences are finding their way into worldwide distribution because the Web makes this practical for the first time. . . .
>
> Bruce Dobler and Harry Bloomberg, "How Much Web Would a Webcourse Weave if a Webcourse Would Weave Webs?" (in *The Dialogic Classroom*, NCTE, 1996).

Forums

Some forum tools are emerging on the Internet. One of these, Net-Forum (http://www.biostat.wisc.edu/nf_home), combines a newsgroup-like bulletin board in a Web interface. Instead of moving between newsgroup and Web, NetForum allows users to stay at the site they are visiting and read through as well as discuss the available resources.

IRCs

Sometimes e-mail can seem too formal, too structured. Also, since senders don't expect receivers of e-mail to be logged in to their computers at the time the message is sent, there can be a considerable time lag between the time a message is sent and the time it is received. Michael Day, a professor at South Dakota School of Mines and Technology, explains his preference for a technology called IRC (Internet Relay Chat): "E-mail may seem too tedious or time-consuming when some participants want to brainstorm or collaborate intensively. . . . [IRC is] like CB or ham radio, except that everyone can talk at once, and everything that is said appears in text" (Galen & Latchaw, 1997). The following box is a brief introduction to IRC that may help you decide if you want to try it.

Internet Relay Chat

What is IRC?

IRC stands for "Internet Relay Chat." IRC is a "chat" program that has many "channels" or discussion areas. IRC gained popularity during the Gulf War when users gathered on a single channel to hear reports. Similarly, during the coup against Boris Yeltsin in September 1993, IRC users from Moscow gave live reports to the world.

An IRC user runs a "client" program (usually called 'irc') which connects to the IRC network via another program called a "server." To see if you have IRC on your system, type "irc" from your login prompt. If you don't have IRC available to you, ask your computer center whether it can be installed.

U.S. SERVERS

irc.bu.edu
irc.colorado.edu
piglet.cc.utexas.edu

CANADIAN SERVERS

irc.mcgill.ca

EUROPEAN SERVERS

irc.funet.fi
cismhp.univ-lyon1.fr
irc.ethz.ch
irc.nada.kth.se
sokrates.informatik.uni-kl.de
bim.itc.univie.ac.at

AUSTRALIAN SERVERS

jello.qabc.uq.oz.au

JAPANESE SERVERS

endo.wide.ad.jp

To join a channel, type < /join #channelname>.
To start talking, type <!>
When you're done with your text, press <return>.
When you choose to leave a channel, just type </part #channel-name>.

A place you might want to listen in on just to get the flavor of an IRC conversation is < #hottub>.

Typing < /list -min 20> will give you a list of 20 channels to choose from. Type a higher or lower number if you wish.

MOOs

Another unusual way to collaborate with research partners is by joining them in a MOO. MOO stands for MUD Object Oriented, and MUD is an acronym for Multi-User Dungeon or, as many prefer, Multi-User Dimension. These environments were created for game playing but have much potential for scholarship. One of the MOOs, MediaMOO, is used by media researchers at MIT and elsewhere. When you log in to MediaMOO, you are assigned a guest name (such as Purple Guest or Cyan Guest). If you are doing media research, you are eligible for a character name. Other MOOs such as Diversity University and Daedalus MOO allow students to work with other participants. It is difficult, of course, to coordinate schedules of people who live in different parts of the world, so meeting synchronously is not always easy.

It's fairly simple to get connected to a MOO. If the MOO has a Web interface, you can access it by entering the http address into your browser's location box. If the MOO you want to reach has a Telnet address, then you will need to have a Telnet program installed on your computer.

Each MOO has its own rules and regulations, so be sure to learn what the guidelines are before you plunge into the conversation.

Here are the addresses of some educational MOOs:

Diversity University
telnet to: moo.du.org:8888
URL:http://www.academic.marist.edu/duwww.htm

Virtual Online University
telnet to: brazos.iac.net:8888
URL:http://www.lac.net/~billp/

Daedalus MOO
telnet to: logos.daedalus.comm:7777

For information about MOOs, consult one of the following sites:

MOO Central
URL:http://www.pitt.edu/~jrgst7/

MSCS-Educational MOOs
URL:http://www.speakeasy.org/~pscs/moo.html

The Lost Library of MOO
URL:http://lucien.sims.berkeley.edu/moo.html

PRACTICE BOX

1. Are you interested in conducting an informal survey for your research project? If so, post the survey to a mailing list dedicated to that topic. If you word your message carefully, you are likely to get some good results.

2. Visit some of the following online writing labs (OWLs) and find out if they feature live MOO chat sessions: Purdue University (http://owl.trc.purdue.edu); Bowling Green (http://www.bgsu.edu/departments/writing-lab/Homepage.html); Michigan State University (http://www. hu.mtu.edu/~jdcolman/wc/welcome.html); Rensselaer Polytechnical Institute (http://www.rpi.edu/dept/llc/writecenter/web/home.html); University of Maine (http://www. ume.maine.edu/~wcenter); Dakota State University (http://www. dsu.edu/departments/liberal/owl/Dakota State). Agree on a specified time and meet with others in your course or students at different schools who are interested in talking about the same topic.

CONCLUSION

You won't become an expert at using e-mail, mailing lists, newsgroups, and other tools for research while working on your first project; and you may not wind up citing any of the comments or ideas that you read. But just by "listening in" on the conversations about your topic you are conducting exploratory research. If you do find information that you want to cite, consult the guidelines in chapter 9 for documenting sources from e-mail, mailing lists, and newsgroups.

END-OF-CHAPTER EXERCISES

1. Subscribe to a list related to your research interests. To find an appropriate mailing list, explore Liszt—Directory of E-mail Discussion Groups (http://www.liszt.com/).
2. Join one or more newsgroups related to your topic. Follow the discussion for several weeks. Take notes on the ways people interact with one another. Note how new topics are introduced, how disagreements are managed, and how newcomers are treated. Examine messages for evidence of shared understandings. Look for common organizational strategies in messages.
3. Discuss the validity of different messages posted to a newsgroup or mailing list. What makes one source better than another? Can you establish the credentials of the authors? How?
4. Learn how to search the archives of the mailing list to which you are subscribed.
5. Use DejaNews, a searchable archive of newsgroups, to search for previous posts about your topic. The address for DejaNews is: http://www.dejanews.com/newusers.html/. A pointer to DejaNews is included on the Net Search page of Netscape.

SUGGESTIONS FOR RESEARCH AND WRITING

A current collection of sources related to these topics can be found at the Web site for this book.

1. Explore uses of e-mail and mailing lists across the country. How are teachers/business executives/students using these tools? What differences are there between e-mail use in one location and in another?
2. Do a research project in which you explore netiquette in at least three different newsgroups with different "net cultures." For example, subscribe to different discipline-based lists or different kinds of newsgroups (recreational, business-related, scholarly). Begin by observing and taking field notes. What issues emerge? How do people address one another? What kinds of language differences do you note? After you have done some groundwork, enter the discussion of the group. If possible, conduct an interview with several individuals in each group.

CHAPTER 8

ORGANIZING RESEARCH NOTES AND SOURCES

One of the biggest advantages of doing research on the Internet is the computer itself. With either a hard drive or with individual disks, you can organize your notes into files and folders and store them for later retrieval and review. You can piece together information from all the sources you've read and rearrange to your heart's delight.

This chapter suggests productive ways of organizing notes and Web sources. First you will learn how to use bookmarks to help you access sources you might want to take notes from or save. Then you will learn how to set up electronic files and folders to keep notes from all your sources: print-based sources such as books and journals as well as online sources, including e-mail messages.

USING BOOKMARKS TO ORGANIZE SOURCES

What are bookmarks? Bookmarks are collections of addresses or URLs of sites you want to revisit. Some browsers, including Netscape, allow you to annotate your bookmarks. By collecting sites that are useful to you, and annotating them, you can turn your bookmark collection into a set of online note cards. By organizing bookmarks carefully into folders and subfolders, your browser can become a personalized writing environment.

In the past, you would have had to photocopy pages if you wanted to avoid taking notes too early in your information-collection process. With the Web, you can use bookmarks to save potentially useful sources. Since you can retrieve your sources readily, you don't need to take notes until you are certain that you will use the source in your paper. Simple bookmarking involves little more than finding a site that you like and clicking on **Add Bookmark.** But if you want to go beyond the basics, you can learn how to organize your bookmark files into folders and subfolders; annotate your bookmarks; set up an organized set of bookmarks and bookmark files; and save your bookmarks as files or reference home pages.

Collecting Bookmarks

If your browser allows it, organize your bookmarks into categories and subcategories—folders and subfolders—as you collect them, taking time to determine what folders are most appropriate for your needs. The procedure for creating hierarchical bookmark files varies with each release of Netscape. Check this book's Web site and locate chapter 8 for directions on different versions.

When you search for sites in a given category, change the menu options so that all the bookmarks for a given subfolder are collected in one spot (see directions in next section). Even a carefully organized set of bookmarks can get unwieldy if you are working on several research projects at once. Netscape allows you to set the bookmark menu to the folder of your choice. Then, as you are looking for sites related to a subtopic of your research, you can establish a new folder and set the menu to that folder. The benefit of this procedure is that as you find sites, you add them to your specific folder rather than to the end of your complete list of bookmarks.

Annotating Bookmarks

Try to get into the habit of bookmarking promising sites and routinely annotating them. By taking the time to jot down a brief description and reaction to each site, your bookmark collection becomes a set of electronic note cards. The annotations remind you of the content as well as the merit of each site.

To annotate a source, select **edit** from the bookmark menu, then type a summary in the "description" section of the screen. Figure 8.1 shows a sample of a bookmark file being annotated. Note that the URL for the source is automatically displayed in the bookmark.

Organizing Bookmarks
and Bookmark Files

With a basic understanding of collecting and annotating bookmarks, you are ready to move into a more creative use of bookmarks—as person-

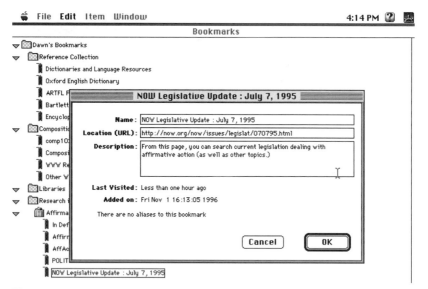

Figure 8.1   Annotating a source using the Edit option on the Bookmark menu.

alized research collections. You can create sets of bookmarks in many ways. Following are suggestions for setting up a set of folders.

1. SET UP A COLLECTION OF FOLDERS FOR RESEARCH PROJECTS.   (You might have other sets of folders for hobbies or volunteer activities.) Figure 8.2 shows an example of the kinds of folders you might set up for your writing and research needs.

2. DETERMINE WHAT CATEGORIES YOU WANT.   Then create a folder for each category. A submenu gives you the choices listed below.

> edit bookmark
> go to bookmark
> sort bookmarks
> insert bookmarks
> insert folder
> insert separator
> set to new bookmarks folder (sites you select will automatically go to the folder you choose)
> set to bookmark menu folder (the bookmark menu will show only the sites you add to this folder)

Select **insert folder** to create each new folder. Then give your folder an appropriate name.

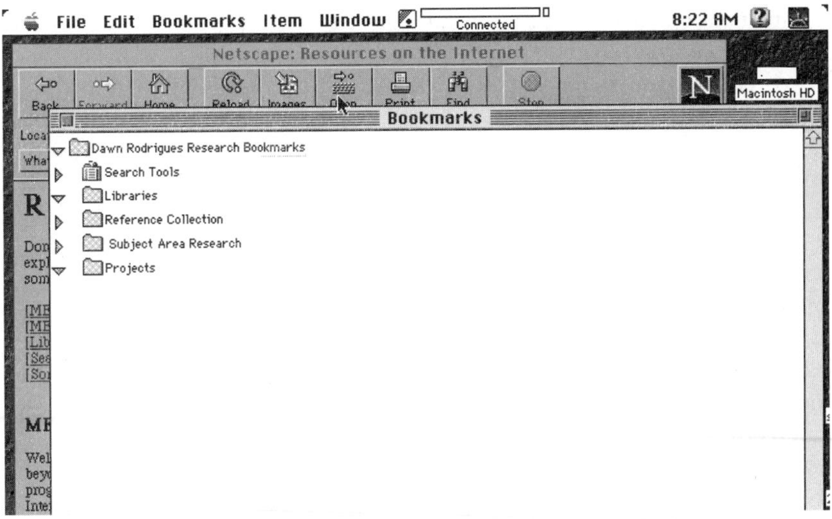

Figure 8.2 Example of folders.

3. COLLECT SITES TO PLACE IN YOUR FOLDER.   For example, if you develop a collection of search tools, you'll be able to access the search sites more quickly than if you depend on using the Net Search button in Netscape. To find sites for your collection, use your favorite search tools. Then bookmark areas that look promising.

Note: As you search for one kind of item for your set of folders, you'll find other sites that you want in your bookmark folder. Go ahead and add to your bookmarks. They will be placed at the end of your current bookmark file. You can move them to the correct folder later. If you want to switch to a new folder you can. Just click on **set to new bookmarks folder** from the selection in the **Item** menu.

Saving Your Bookmarks as Files or Reference Home Pages

You may want to save your bookmarks for each research project to a separate file. Then, instead of having an intricate hierarchy of bookmarks, with annotations buried within the bookmark editor, you can convert your bookmarks to a local file—a home page of sorts—and view or print your notes. If you save your files on a computer disk, you can take the disk with you to a computer classroom or lab.

Your bookmarks are automatically saved as an HTML file every time you exit your browser. Netscape automatically names the file in a way that Netscape can recognize as a bookmark file. If you want to use your bookmarks as a local home page, you should save your bookmarks with a new name, thus leaving your original bookmarks intact. Save your bookmarks as a file. Follow the directions provided with your version of Netscape. You have the option of saving your file as text or as source code (HTML). Save your file as source code. Give it a descriptive name such as "Research Bookmarks."

To use your file as a home page, select **Open File** from the Netscape main menu. Then select the appropriate file and the bookmark file will appear in your browser. (Any home page on the Web can be saved as a file on your computer or floppy disk and used later as a home page.)

Why would you want to view your bookmark collection as a local file? When loaded as a local file, you see not only your bookmarked sites, but your annotations, too. Your "home page" can have annotations and be kept in a research notebook. How does this happen? The HTML code that is saved includes commands that direct your browser to insert the annotations into the space below each site's name. Any time you want to use your file as a standard set of bookmarks, just select **import** from the bookmark editing menu in Netscape. You can then adapt your local file in any way you want. If you load your files into a word processing program, you can add more text to the annotations. (If you modify your file, save it with a new name so that you can preserve your original set of bookmarks.)

A good example of the technique of turning bookmark files into home pages can be found on the Web. The Berkeley Public Library routinely collects useful bookmarks and turns them into Web pages using this technique (see figure 8.3). After the librarians create the home page by collecting bookmarks, they save that page in source code (using the same technique described earlier) and they place their finished page on their Web site for others to access. If you visit their site, you can save the home page in source code and use it as a local home page. You can also import the file into your bookmark collection, edit the bookmark folders, and integrate them into your own bookmark collection (see figure 8.4).

PRACTICE BOX

1. Discuss ways of organizing bookmark collections for different purposes. Develop a plan for your own collection.

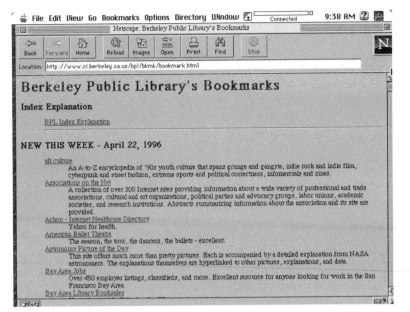

Figure 8.3   Berkeley Public Library Web page constructed by loading a file created with bookmarks.   Copyright 1996 Netscape Communications Corp. All rights reserved. This page may not be reprinted or copied without the express written permission of Netscape.

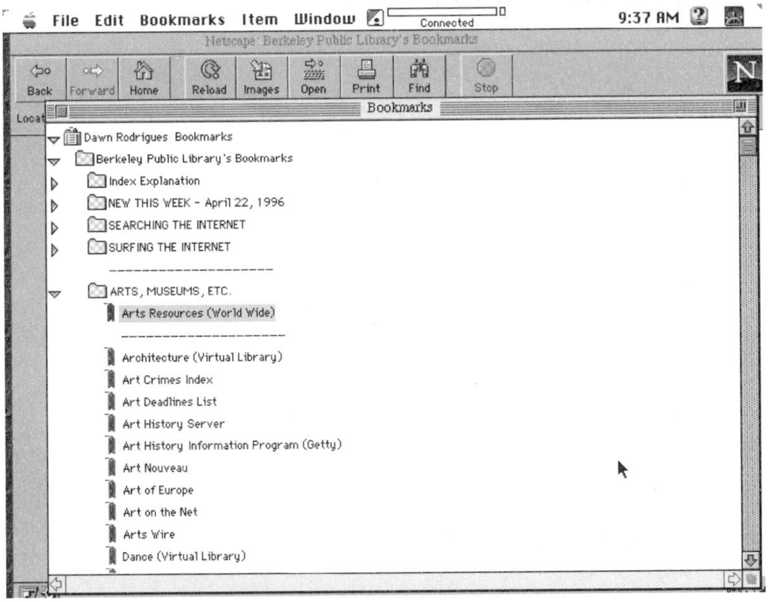

Figure 8.4   Bookmark collection before having been saved as a local file.
Copyright 1996 Netscape Communications Corp. All rights reserved. This page may not be reprinted or copied without th express written permission of Netscape.

> 2. Create a set of bookmarks for your general research needs. Share your bookmarks with classmates and/or colleagues at work using the techniques described in this chapter. Consider posting your bookmark collections as part of your Web page. Even though you create bookmark collections for your own needs, others might be able to modify them for their research.

SETTING UP YOUR ELECTRONIC WORK SPACE

Take time to organize an effective electronic workspace by establishing file structures with your word processing program, or through a separate utility program. If you have your own computer, establish a separate folder with several subfolders for your research project. Even if you do not have your own computer, try to think through ways of organizing your files into folders on a disk. Use that disk or set of disks exclusively for your research project. Although you need to refine the technique described in this section to suit your own workstyle, some version of it may be useful to you.

Here are the kinds of files and folders to consider establishing (see figure 8.5):

1. A folder for your research project.
2. A **research notebook** folder or file—where you keep dated notes about your research and writing process.
3. A set of **subtopic folders**—where you copy notes that fit subdivisions of your topic. In most cases, you won't think of many subtopics until late in your research process. As a new subtopic occurs to you, just create a new subfolder to store your information.
4. A folder or file that serves as a combination **note card/bibliography card** file—with "template" note cards that you use to take notes from your sources (either typing in notes from print sources or pasting in portions of online sources).
5. A **draft** file—to write your research project draft.

Research Project Folder

This folder holds subfolders for all work related to a designated research project, including e-mail notes and bibliography entries as well as drafts of the research paper itself.

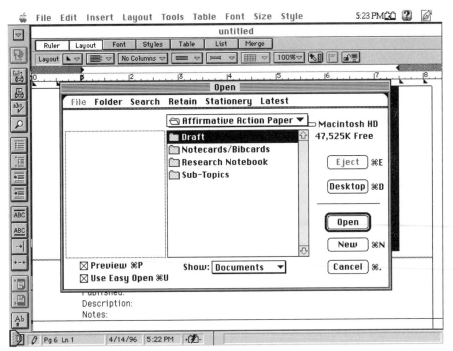

Figure 8.5   Research paper folder and subtopic folders.

Subtopic folders.   Subtopic folders can serve many purposes. Some files in the subtopic folder can be Gopher or Web pages that you have saved as a unit (see figure 8.6). Other files may be e-mail messages that you have moved to this folder. Still another file may be a collection of note cards on this topic that you have copied from your primary note card file along with note cards that you create as you take notes from your Web and e-mail files.

If you include a file for your draft, another file for research notes, and another set of files for notes on subtopics then you can move easily between your draft file and your various note files.

Research Notebook Folder.   The research notes file (see figure 8.7) will help you write reminders to yourself. It's particularly important to write down what you were doing as you ended your writing session so that you can take up when you begin again.

Your research notebook might also include a chart in which you evaluate your sources. Here's a sample of what such a chart might look like:

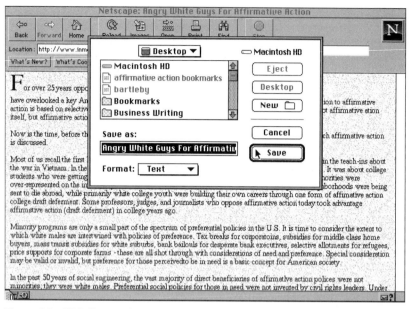

Figure 8.6 Web file saved as a file.

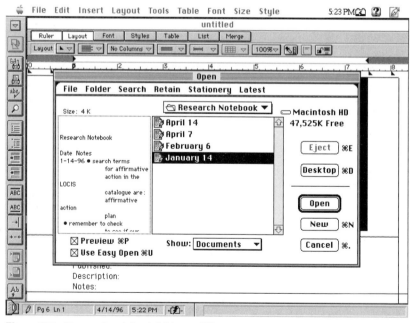

Figure 8.7 Research notebook folder and files.

Source	Library location of source	Internet location of source	Value of source good (*) promising (**) excellent (***)

PRACTICE BOX

1. Since each word processing program is slightly different, develop a way of organizing files and folders that will work for your program. How do you insert an existing file into a file you are using? Be ready to share your strategy and technical solutions with others who may use the same word processing package.

2. Practice capturing your library searches to a file so you can incorporate the results into note card and bibliography files.

3. Develop an alternative way of organizing your electronic work area.

Electronic Note Cards

Create an electronic note card file for note taking. Design a "template" or form to use in your note card file. Use the categories shown in figure 8.8 or similar ones to record your notes. After you design your note card, copy it about ten times so that you have a set of blank template note cards. Continue copying your entire set until you have a file of about fifty or more cards.

To design a master template file, follow these steps:

1. Open a new file with your word processor.

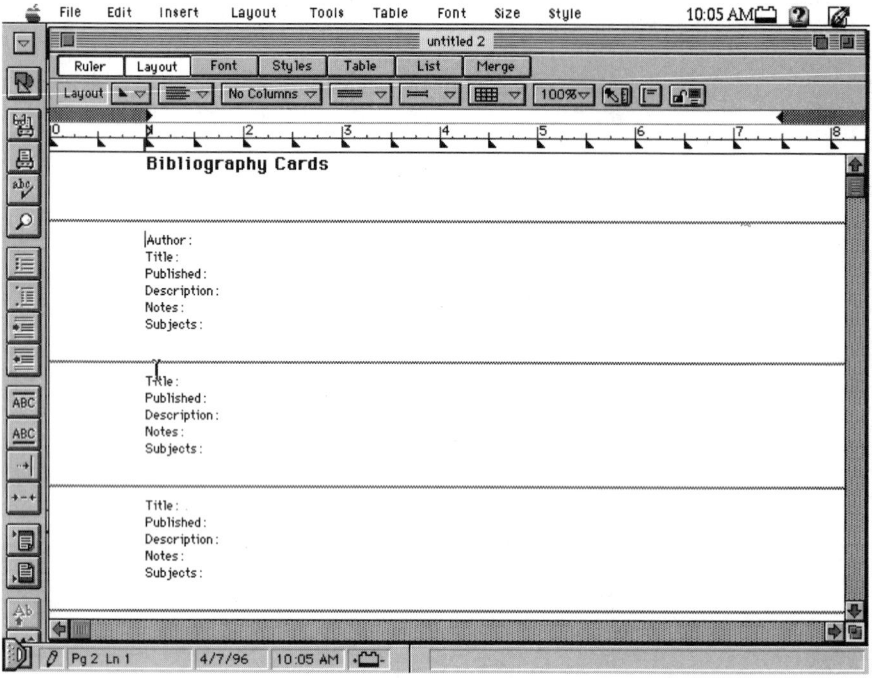

Figure 8.8   Bibliography/note card template file.

2. Type the categories you want to use. Do not fill them in.
3. Save the file with an identifiable name, such as bib.temp for a bibliography template.

To use the template file:

1. Load the master template file (e.g., bib.temp).
2. Use the Save As feature of your word processor to give the file a new name (e.g., Literature.bib). Note: If you don't re-name the file you will be over-writing your master file.

If you design your bibliography cards to match the way your library presents the results of library searches, then you can copy and paste results of your library search to your bibliography file. You will need to know how to turn the capture feature on your computer on and off so that you can preserve the results of a library search for later editing.

Consider developing a system for note taking. In the example in figure 8.9, the student used a script font to indicate notes that he took in his own words and a bold font to indicate snippets of text that he cut and pasted into the note card.

Even though you may not decide to quote portions of text that you place on your note card, the ease of copying and pasting makes it possible to have exact words of an author easily at your disposal. As long as you are careful to avoid plagiarism, you should use the power that technology affords you.

Author: Bill Bradley
Title: Ending Racism Can Never Be Just About Numbers
Published: Los Angeles Times   Monday, January 15, 1996
          Home Edition
          Metro, Page 5
Description: Type of Material: Opinion; Transcript

Notes: *This is from a speech Bradley gave. Bradley feels that the issue is discrimination and it had been that since the 60s. The assumption is that if we could get rid of racism we could have a* **"spiritually transformed America."**

Bradley says that instead of talking about getting rid of affirmative action we should focus on getting people from all racial backgrounds to interact more with one another:
A new political vision requires people to engage each other, endure the pain, learn from each other's history, absorb each other's humanity and move on to higher ground. It won't happen overnight, nor will one person bring it, however illustrative his career, nor will one person destroy it, however heinous his crime or poisonous his rhetoric.
Subjects: RACISM

Author: Slater, Robert Bruce
Title: Why Socioeconomic Affirmative Action in College Admissions Works Against African Americans
Published: Journal of Blacks in Higher Education, The, 06-30-1995, pp PG.
Description:
Notes: *The author notes that the number of blacks at many schools would go down dramatically if socioeconomic status were used instead of race and ethnicity.*
Quote:
First, they found that if all selections were based on academic standing and standardized test scores alone, the percentage of blacks in the freshman class would drop from 6 percent to between 0.5 percent and 1.9 percent. White enrollment would rise by as much as 25 percent from its present level of 29.8 percent of Berkeley's freshman class. Asian enrollment, which was 41.7 percent of the 1994 entering freshman class,

---

Figure 8.9   Sample bibliography card/note card file with student's notes in script and quoted text in boldface.

Sometimes you will want to type directly into your template file. Other times you will copy into your file portions of text that you are considering quoting.

If you have saved Web pages to separate files, you may wish to open the Web page in one window of your word processor and your note card/bibliography card file in another so that you can take notes, switching from the text of your Web file to your note card.

Draft File

Open a separate file to draft your paper. If you keep your note cards file (and selected sub-topic files) open as you draft, you can move between files as you write. Many authors also create an outline file to guide them as they work.

OTHER ORGANIZATIONAL STRATEGIES

Capturing Online Sessions

If you access the Web by e-mail or by remote login, you may need to capture to disk in order to save the results of your work. In particular, if you look at library holdings, you may want to have a list of all the sources you view online. Here's what you do:

1. Turn on the capture feature of your communications software. (This tells your computer to save everything that you view to a special file that you can later retrieve and edit.)
2. If you are viewing a lot of information, turn capture on and off as you go. (Some capture files add new information to the end of the file; be sure that you don't "write over" existing information.)
3. At a later point, open both your capture and your note card file and then incorporate any useful information into your notes file.

Let's assume that you decide to check to see whether an UnCover search will produce useful results. Here's what you would do:

1. Access UnCover.
2. Begin searching.
3. Turn capture on.
4. Scroll through the screens you want to save.
5. Turn capture off.

Later, you can retrieve the file and incorporate the data into your note card file. Or you could save it to a subtopic folder for later use.

Sending Yourself E-mail as You Explore the Web

Netscape allows you to send the text of the page you are viewing to your e-mail address. This is particularly handy if you are in the library or computer lab using a Web browser. If you use e-mail from within Netscape, you can attach any Web page to an e-mail message and then retrieve the message at your own computer. When you retrieve the file, be sure to save it to an appropriate subfolder.

PRACTICE BOX

1. How do you save to different folders in your e-mail program? Learn the steps and write them in the back cover of this book.

2. Create several folders in your e-mail program. How do you move the notes in these folders to a directory in your word processor? Discuss this with your classmates or colleagues.

3. Do a brief survey via e-mail. Ask peers or participants in a mailing list to indicate whether they use their e-mail program to categorize and sort data. If so, ask them to describe their techniques. Offer to post the results of your survey to the group. Be sure to design your survey so that e-mail respondents can complete it easily. Suggest that respondents include your message in their reply. Then they can complete your survey online. Put items that can be checked with an x in the left-hand column so that they can be completed easily. When respondents return the survey, use e-mail folders to organize the responses. For example, you might put responses from professors in one folder and responses from students in a composition course in another folder. Here's a sample of how you might format a survey question:

I sort notes in my e-mail folder:

[ ] always

[ ] sometimes

[ ] never

Save open-ended items for the end of the survey so that you can easily identify them.

Taking Notes from Mailing Lists

As you read through your messages from mailing lists, save those that seem to connect with your paper topic. Take time to learn how to organize your e-mail into folders. (If you can save directly to disk, do so; if you have to save to your account on a UNIX machine, then you need to learn how to download or capture to disk so that you can edit the file and put it into your electronic note card collection.)

With all of your saved files in marked subtopic folders, you'll be ready to copy portions of your messages into your main note card file. If you keep your notes organized, then when you are ready to start outlining or drafting your paper, you can easily read through your collection of notes in your note card file to see what you've gathered on your topic.

Using Portions of E-mail Messages in Note Cards

If you save your e-mail messages to folders, you'll need to read through your messages and decide what portions to cut and paste to your note card folder.

The two-step process is as follows:

Step One: Save e-mail messages to a subtopic folder in your e-mail program. When you reread the files, you can highlight the portions you think are worth copying to your note card file. Note the highlighted portion of the e-mail message below:

```
Return-Path: <nii-teach@wais.com>
Received: from wais.wais.com by kscsuna1.Kennesaw.Edu (4.1/SMI-4.1)
  id AA09674; Wed, 6 Apr 94 18:52:31 EDT
Received: from ([127.0.0.1]) by wais.wais.com (4.1/SMI-4.1/Brent-911016)
  id AA29920; Wed, 6 Apr 94 15:43:25 PDT
Date: Wed, 6 Apr 94 15:43:25 PDT
Message-Id: <199404062241.AA21429@ux1.cso.uiuc.edu>
Reply-To: nii-teach@wais.com
Originator: nii-teach@scholastic.com
Sender: nii-teach@wais.com
Precedence: bulk
From: sandberg@ux1.cso.uiuc.edu (Philip Sandberg)
To: Multiple recipients of list <nii-teach@wais.com>
Subject: University-School Internet Synergism
X-Listprocessor-Version: 6.0b — ListProcessor by Anastasios Kotsikonas
```

Recent comments by Paul Brady (in Nutrition Science at the Univ. of Minnesota) have prompted me to enter the discussion on technology and teacher education.

 University faculty members can contribute not only to teachers-in-training, but also to the practicing classroom teachers.

**Communicating electronically can produce collaborations with
very distant classrooms and teachers of quite varied levels of
sophistication. By collaborating with them in Internet projects,
the educational objectives of both the K-12 teacher and the
university professor can be advanced. The university faculty
member can serve as a "subject-matter expert" accessible
either independently, or through some brokered system such
as the "Talk to the Experts" one that Judith Harris at the
University of Texas is running. Even the students in a general
education course can serve as "apprentice-experts" supplying
answers to questions from school classrooms and teachers.
This latter approach is the one I have used in Project
GEO-HELP with my students in "History of Life."**

I think it is important for individuals outside of education and
computer science who have even basic competency in educational
technology to come forward and take part. From my experience here at
UIUC, I don't foresee that universities are going to start offering an
electronic literacy course equivalent to introductory rhetoric any time soon,
although that is the breadth of coverage and level of commitment that is
really needed if students (including those in education) are to be
enfranchised to make use of the NII and educational electronic media. We
don't have to start with multimedia and Mosaic... A great deal can be done
with simple e-mail, and a surprisingly large number of schools and teachers
are on the network. They are at all stages of the learning process, just like
those of us in universities. We can do a lot to help one another and to
expand the educational horizons of both university and K-12 students. For
example, there are certainly many classrooms interested in diet, nutrition,
and other Food Science issues that would love to have Paul Brady and his
students as a resource. My students, who are only about 20% education
majors are having a wonderful time helping school students from 2nd grade
to high school with answers to questions on the history of the earth and
life on earth. Your students could have the same kind of mentoring role and
enriching experience.

Step Two: Put the segment of the file that seems like a possible quote
into a file in your note card folder. Because standards for documenting
electronic sources keep changing, it's a good idea to copy and paste as much
of the address as you might need in the future.

Author: Philip Sandberg
Source:
Return-Path: <nii-teach@wais.com>
Received: from wais.wais.com by kscsuna1.Kennesaw.Edu (4.1/SMI-4.1)
 id AA09674; Wed, 6 Apr 94 18:52:31 EDT
 From: sandberg@ux1.cso.uiuc.edu (Philip Sandberg)
To: Multiple recipients of list <nii-teach@wais.com>
Subject: University-School Internet Synergism
X-Listprocessor-Version: 6.0b — ListProcessor by Anastasios Kotsikonas

QUOTE FROM SOURCE:
**Communicating electronically can produce collaborations with very distant
classrooms and teachers of quite varied levels of sophistication. By
collaborating with them in Internet projects, the educational objectives of
both the K-12 teacher and the university professor can be advanced. The**

university faculty member can serve as a "subject-matter expert" accessible either independently, or through some brokered system such as the "Talk to the Experts" one that Judith Harris at the University of Texas is running. Even the students in a general education course can serve as "apprentice-experts" supplying answers to questions from school classrooms and teachers. This latter approach is the one I have used in Project GEO-HELP with my students in "History of Life."

CONCLUSION

This chapter has suggested some ways to organize the notes and quotations that you find as you investigate your topic. As you try these techniques, adapt them to your own context: different browsers, different e-mail programs, and different word processing programs will all suggest different possibilities for organization. Use whatever strategies work best for your needs. What matters is not *how* you organize your Web-based notes and traditional resources, but *that* you organize them in a way uniquely suited to your writing process and your research project.

END-OF-CHAPTER EXERCISES

1. Keep a log of the most effective ways you have discovered for organizing your Internet-related research notes. Post these ideas to the Web site for this text.
2. Consider partnering with an elementary school. The students in the school can be your tele-mentors if they happen to have significant Web expertise. You can be their writing tutors.

SUGGESTIONS FOR RESEARCH AND WRITING

A current collection of sources related to these topics can be found at the Web site for this book.

1. Do a project on how computers are changing writers' ways of writing and conducting research. You might want to interview writers, librarians, and on-the-job researchers.
2. The Internet is creating new kinds of careers, some of which involve working out of the home: Web-meisters (creators of Web pages); Web designers; online career specialists; Internet business specialists. For your research project, see if you can learn more about such issues as the availability of these careers, the satisfaction level of home-based employees, or the qualifications needed to land a new kind of Internet position.
3. The nature of research is changing. Do a project in which you make predictions for the future, based on your investigation into past and present ways of conducting research. (Some suggestions for getting started: Do some pre-

liminary reading about ways archivists in Mesopotamia worked together in great halls as they gathered cuneiform tablets to preserve the history of their civilization. Examine the role of the printing press in the development of literacy. Explore Internet sites to see how researchers are collaborating today.

CHAPTER 9

DOCUMENTING SOURCES

Research has to be documented. What this means is that as a researcher you need to explain your research techniques and present the results; it also means that you must show readers how you came to your conclusions. To do that, you must provide correct bibliographic citations for the sources you use.

Readers should be able to understand how your sources support your line of argument or your interpretation of evidence. Readers should also be able to locate the sources themselves so that they can judge their reliability and validity firsthand if they so desire. (See chapter 1 for a discussion of validity of sources.)

The term *documenting sources* refers to the process of keeping track of your information and citing it properly in your completed research report. This chapter reviews the basics of documentation style, provides you with a sample paper, then turns to issues involved in Internet and Web citation.

DIFFERENT CITATION STYLES IN DIFFERENT DISCIPLINES

Specialists in different disciplines have worked together over the years to establish conventions for citing sources in their respective disciplines. When you write papers for different courses, you should find out what documentation style your professor wants you to use. This chapter covers the Modern Language Association style (MLA), which is used in the humanities, and the American Psychological Association style (APA), which is most often used by the social sciences. Other fields use different style guides.

Check the Web site for this chapter for information on using style guides in other fields of study.

You may think it would make more sense if all disciplines simply followed the same guidelines. Maybe it would. But there are reasons why different disciplines prefer different citation styles. Scholars in the social sciences, for example, are more interested in the date a work was published than are humanists. Thus, a standard reference to a book in MLA style refers to the author and page number in the internal citation (e.g., Rodrigues 36) whereas a similar citation in APA style for a science or a social science course would provide the date (e.g., Rodrigues 1996).

Here is a brief overview of the two documentation styles covered in this book: MLA style calls for a source name and a page reference for internal citations (in-text) and a Works Cited list at the end of the paper; APA style calls for a source name, year, and if you have an exact quote, a page reference for in-text citations and a References list at the end of the paper.

The style and format for the research paper itself varies from one discipline to the next. Humanities research papers are written in an essay style, whereas social sciences and science papers use report format, with headings and subheadings often included. Check with your instructor for specific guidelines.

INTERNAL CITATION AND BIBLIOGRAPHIC CITATION

To properly document a research paper, you must use two types of citations: internal citations within the body of your paper and bibliographic citations listed at the end of your paper.

Internal or in-text citations in parentheses provide the key publication information about sources you have quoted from, paraphrased, or summarized. The purpose of a parenthetical in-text citation is to acknowledge the information source and to refer the reader to the list of bibliographic citations at the end of your paper. The bibliographic citations, arranged into a list alphabetized by author names, provide all of the pertinent publication information about the sources referred to in internal citations. This list is given different names in different documentation styles: in MLA it is called Works Cited, while in APA it is called References.

Here are some important aspects of in-text citation, which replaces the outmoded style of using footnotes at the bottom of pages:

1. **If you refer to the author in your sentence, do not repeat the author's name in the parenthesis.**

MLA: In *The Research Paper and the World Wide Web*, Rodrigues discusses ways to link Internet research and standard library research.

APA: In *The Research Paper and the World Wide Web* (1997), Rodrigues discusses ways to link Internet research and standard library research.

Only the page numbers being referred to are needed in an MLA citation. No internal citation is needed for the APA example, because APA does not require a specific page reference unless you are using a direct quotation. Note: If you are referring to the entire book rather than to a specific section, then you may need *no* parenthetical citation, since the reader can refer to the author's name in the Works Cited list.

2. **If you do not refer to the author's name in your sentence, then you must include the author's name in parenthesis.**

MLA: In *The Research Paper and the World Wide Web*, the author discusses ways to link Internet research and standard library research (Rodrigues).

APA: *The Research Paper and the World Wide Web* (Rodrigues, 1997) presents ways to link Internet research and standard library research.

GUIDELINES FOR INTERNAL CITATIONS

Documentation should be used sparingly and skillfully. Don't just collect a disorganized array of sources and quote them at random. Instead, organize the points you want to make and then refer to your sources by integrating them into the flow of your argument. Remember to use "tag" lines such as the following:

- As the author notes, ...
- Another author disagrees. Harris says that [paraphrase of source] . . . .
- In her book on [subject], Rodrigues writes . . . .

Consider the following ways the author of the MLA paper excerpted later in this chapter has incorporated sources and how the sources would be cited in APA style:

1. Paraphrasing an Indirect Source

MLA: President Lyndon Johnson issued Executive Order 11246 calling for "affirmative action" among federal contractors, colleges, universities, and the federal government. The intent of this order was to increase the numbers of minorities and women in colleges, universities, and federal programs (qtd. in Lappe 97).

APA: President Lyndon Johnson issued Executive Order 11246 calling for "affirmative action" among federal contractors, colleges, universities, and the federal government. The intent of this order was to increase the numbers of minorities and women in colleges, universities, and federal programs (qtd. in Lappe, 1995).

2. Using a Block Quotation

MLA: He explained the need for affirmative action in a June 1965 address at Howard University, noting that freedom of opportunity doesn't immediately level the playing field.

> You do not take a man who for years has been hobbled by chains, liberate him, bring him to the starting line of a race, saying 'you are free to compete with all others,' and still justly believe you have been completely fair. Thus it is not enough to open the gates of opportunity. (qtd. in Lappe 97)

APA: He explained the need for affirmative action in a June 1965 address at Howard University, noting that freedom of opportunity doesn't immediately level the playing field.

> You do not take a man who for years has been hobbled by chains, liberate him, bring him to the starting line of a race, saying 'you are free to compete with all others,' and still justly

believe you have been completely fair. Thus it is not enough to open the gates of opportunity. (qtd. in Lappe, 1995, p. 97)

3. Quoting a Complete Sentence from a Source

MLA: As Pedro Noguera points out, "Without a policy that holds universities and employers accountable for who they admit, the pledge to not discriminate is meaningless" (50).

APA: As Pedro Noguera (1996) points out, "Without a policy that holds universities and employers accountable for who they admit, the pledge to not discriminate is meaningless" (p. 50).

4. Identifying the Origin of a Source Without Quoting It

MLA: A study done found that students from all racial and ethnic groups showed strong support for diversity efforts in the curriculum (Lopez 33).

APA: A study done found that students from all racial and ethnic groups showed strong support for diversity efforts in the curriculum (Lopez, 1995).

5. Quoting Only a Few Words from a Source

MLA: Some groups argue that affirmative action isn't really needed in some parts of the country. One group of students at the University of California (Students Against Affirmative Action and for Equality) has argued that diversity would exist on their campus without what they see as offensive "racially based guidelines," since they live in a place with a mix of cultures (Greenman).

APA: Some groups argue that affirmative action isn't really needed in some parts of the country. One group of students at the University of California (Students Against Affirmative Action and for Equality) has argued that diversity would exist on their campus without what they see as offensive "racially based guidelines," since they live in a place with a mix of cultures (Greenman, 1996).

6. Quoting a Portion of a Sentence

MLA: Columnist Bill Bradley is convinced that racism and discrimination won't go away easily because "many people hold values that allow them to defend the social advantage they have based on being upper class whites" (10).

APA: Columnist Bill Bradley (1996) is convinced that racism and discrimination won't go away easily because "many people hold values that allow them to defend the social advantage they have based on being upper class whites" (p. 10).

7. Introducing a Source with "Tag" Words (Such as "As X Argues")

MLA: As R. Richard Banks argues, there is an increasing reluctance of intellectuals and politicians to identify social problems as explicitly racial problems (45).

APA: As R. Richard Banks (1995) argues, there is an increasing reluctance of intellectuals and politicians to identify social problems as explicitly racial problems.

8. Summarizing an Entire Source

MLA: Richard Kalenberg offers a choice of several ways to address class rather than race in college admissions, ranging from a simple reporting of family income to a more complex series of calculations based on factors such as the neighborhood where a student lives, the quality of the high school that he or she may have attended, and family income.

APA: Richard Kalenberg (1995) offers a choice of several ways to address class rather than race in college admissions, ranging from a simple reporting of family income to a more complex series of calculations based on factors such as the neighborhood where a student lives, the quality of the high school that he or she may have attended, and family income.

9. Using a Combination of Methods

MLA: Banks feels that both race and class have to be factored in, even though race matters more. In "Race Matters More," he maintains that proposals to base affirmative action on economic class alone rather than on race ignore fundamental truths about the interplay of race and class (32). Banks feels that if we really cared about helping others, we'd come up with ways of factoring both race and class into affirmative action programs. His point is that it is illogical to think that helping poor people equates with helping black people. He sees the whole attempt to focus on class alone as a way of skirting the real issue—an inability to "confront the depth of our racial difficulties. (32)" He notes that blacks who are poor have difficulty competing in society not only because of their poverty but also because of their color. He does not think that "remediating class disparities will dissolve our racial difficulties. . ." (33).

APA: Banks (1996) feels that both race and class have to be factored in, even though race matters more. In "Race Matters More," he maintains that proposals to base affirmative action on economic class alone rather than on race ignore fundamental truths about the interplay of race and class. Banks feels that if we really cared about helping others, we'd come up with ways of factoring both race and class into affirmative action programs. His point is that it is illogical to think that helping poor people equates with helping black people. He sees the whole attempt to focus on class alone as a way of skirting the real issue—an inability to "confront the depth of our racial difficulties. (32)" He notes that blacks who are poor have difficulty competing in society not only because of their poverty but also because of their color. He does not think that "remediating class disparities will dissolve our racial difficulties. . . ." (p. 33)

GUIDELINES
FOR BIBLIOGRAPHIC
CITATIONS

Refer to the following pages for quick reference to citation guidelines. For more detailed guidelines, consult the official style guide of either the Modern Language Association or the American Psychological Association. For links to summaries of these guides, consult the Web site for this chapter.

1. Book by One Author

MLA: Chandrasekhar, S. *Hungry People and Empty Lands: An Essay on Population Problems and International Tensions.* London: G. Allen & Unwin, 1954.

APA: Chandrasekhar, S. (1954). *Hungry people and empty lands: An essay on population problems and international tensions.* London: G. Allen & Unwin.

2. Book by Two or Three Authors

MLA: Loescher, Gil, and John A. Scanlan. *Calculated Kindness: Refugees and America's Half-Open Door, 1945 to the Present.* New York: The Free Press, 1986.

APA: Loescher, G., & Scanlan, J. A. (1986). *Calculated kindness: Refugees and America's half-open door, 1945 to the present.* New York: The Free Press.

3. Two or More Books by the Same Author(s)

MLA: Nugent, Walter T. K. *Crossings: The Great Transatlantic Migrations, 1870-1914.* Bloomington: Indiana UP, 1992.
         ---. *Structures of American Social History.* Bloomington: Indiana UP, 1981.
         ---. *The Tolerant Populists: Kansas, Populism and Nativism.* Chicago: U of Chicago P, 1963.

APA: Nugent, W. T. K. (1963). *The tolerant populists: Kansas, populism and nativism.* Chicago: University of Chicago Press.

Nugent, W. T. K. (1981). *Structures of American social history.* Bloomington, IN: Indiana University Press.

Nugent, W. T. K. (1992). *Crossings: The great transatlantic migrations, 1870-1914.* Bloomington, IN: Indiana University Press.

4. Book by Group or Corporate Author

MLA: International Labour Office. *Migration in Its Various Forms.* Geneva: ILO, 1926.

APA: International Labour Office. (1926). *Migration in its various forms.* Geneva: ILO.

5. Translation

MLA: Avni, Haim. *Argentina and the Jews: A History of Jewish Immigration.* Trans. G. Brand. Tuscaloosa, AL: U of Alabama P, 1991.

APA: Avni, H. (1991). Argentina and the Jews: A history of Jewish immigration. (G. Brand, Trans.). Tuscaloosa, AL: University of Alabama Press.

6. Signed Article in a Reference Book

MLA: Scott, Franklin D. "Immigration." *The Encyclopedia Americana.* 1993 ed.

APA: Scott, F.D. (1993). Immigration. In *The encyclopedia Americana.* (International ed.) (Vol. 14, pp. 803-808). Danbury, CT: Grolier.

7. Unsigned Article in a Reference Book

MLA: "Refugee." *The New Encyclopedia Britannica.* 1991 ed.

APA: Refugee. (1991). In *The new encyclopedia Britannica* (14th ed.) (Vol. 9, p. 998). Chicago: Encyclopedia Britannica.

8. Introduction, Preface, Foreword, or Afterword

MLA: Glazer, Nathan. Introduction. *Clamor at the Gates: The New American Immigration.* By Glazer. San Francisco: Institute for Contemporary Studies, 1985. 3-13.
Rossant, M. J. Foreword. *Closed Borders: The Contemporary Assault on Freedom of Movement.* By Alan Dowty. New Haven: Yale UP, 1987, ix-x.

APA: Glazer, N. (1985). Introduction. In *Clamor at the gates: The new American immigration.* (pp. 3-13). San Francisco: Institute for Contemporary Studies.
Rossant, M. J. (1987). Foreword. In A. Dowty, *Closed borders: The contemporary assault on freedom of movement.* (pp. ix-x). New Haven: Yale University Press.

9. Government Publications

MLA: United States. Immigration and Naturalization Service. Office of Policy and Planning. *Strategic Plan: Toward INS 2000: Accepting the Challenge.* Washington: GPO, 1994.

APA: Immigration and Naturalization Service. (1994). *Strategic plan: Toward INS 2000: Accepting the challenge.* Washington, DC: Government Printing Office.

10. Signed Article from a Daily Newspaper

MLA: Jouzaitis, Carol. "GOP, Business Split on Immigration Issue." *Chicago Tribune* 27 Feb. 1996: 4.

APA: Jouzaitis, C. (1994, February 27). GOP, business split on immigration issue. *The Chicago Tribune,* p. 4.

11. Editorial, Letter to the Editor, Review

MLA: "Don't Bar All Immigrants." Editorial. *USA Today* 29 Feb. 1996: A11.
Altshuler, Linda. "Barnum Didn't Say It." Letter. *New York Times* 15 July 1996: A12.

Wolfe, Alan. "Displaced Persons." Rev. of *Fresh Blood*
by Sanford J. Ungar and *American Dreaming:
Immigrant Life on the Margins* by Sarah J. Mahler.
New York Times Book Review 17 Dec. 1995: 29.

APA: Don't bar all immigrants. (1996, February 29).
[Editorial]. *USA Today,* p. A11.
     Altshuler, L. (1996, July 15). Barnum didn't say
it. [Letter to the editor]. *The New York Times,* p.
A12.
     Wolfe, A. (1995, December 17). Displaced Persons.
[Review of the books *Fresh blood* & *American dreaming:
Immigrant life on the margins*]. *The New York Times
Book Review,* p. 29.

12. Unsigned Article from a Daily Newspaper

MLA: "Tech Firms Oppose a Ban on Immigrants." *USA Today* 28
Feb. 1996: B4.

APA: Tech Firms Oppose a Ban on Immigrants. (1996,
February 28). *USA Today,* p. B4.

13. Signed Article from a Weekly Magazine

MLA: Smith, Norman. "Bosnian Asylum-Seekers Targeted by
Home Office." *New Statesman & Society* 24 Nov.
1995: 9.

APA: Smith, N. (1995, November 24). Bosnian asylum-
seekers targeted by home office. *New Statesman &
Society,* 9.

14. Signed Article from a Monthly or Bimonthly Periodical

MLA: Lequerica, Martha. "Stress in Immigrant Families with
Handicapped Children: A Child Advocacy Approach."
American Journal of Orthopsychiatry Oct. 1993:
545-52.
Weiner, Myron. "Nations Without Borders: The Gifts of
Folk Gone Abroad." *Foreign Affairs* Mar.-Apr.
1996: 128-34.

APA: Lequerica, M. (1993, October). Stress in immigrant
families with handicapped children: A child advocacy
approach. *American Journal of Orthopsychiatry*, 545-52.
        Weiner, M. (1996, March/April). Nations without
borders: The gifts of folk gone abroad. *Foreign
Affairs*, 128-34.

15. Unsigned Article from a Weekly or Monthly Periodical

MLA: "No Room at Europe's Inn." *The Economist* 9 Dec. 1995:
53-54.

APA: No Room at Europe's Inn. (1995, December 9). *The
Economist,* pp. 53-54.

16. Article in a Journal with Continuous Pagination

MLA: Massey, Douglas S. "The New Immigration and Ethnicity
in the United States." *Population and Development
Review* 21 (1995): 631-52.

APA: Massey, D. S. (1995). The new immigration and
ethnicity in the United States. *Population and
Development Review, 21,* 631-652.

17. Article in a Journal That Pages Each Issue Separately

MLA: McKelvey, Robert S., and John A. Webb. "Unaccompanied
Status as a Risk Factor in Vietnamese
Amerasians." *Social Science & Medicine* 41.2
(1995): 261-66.

APA: McKelvey, R. S., & Webb, J. A. (1995).
Unaccompanied status as a risk factor in Vietnamese
Amerasians. *Social Science & Medicine, 41*(2), 261-266.

GUIDELINES FOR ELECTRONIC CITATIONS

The best way to begin learning how to cite electronic sources is to realize
that they follow the same general principles for in-text citation and works
cited that are used for print sources in your field. That is, MLA electronic

citations follow the guidelines for MLA books and journals, with only slight adaptations for the special requirements of the Internet. Similarly, APA guidelines are the starting point for the electronic citations that follow APA style. The goal is to give the author credit and to help the reader find the source, which means, in most cases, indicating either the URL address that has to be entered to access the resource or the publication information for other electronic media such as CD-ROMs or videodiscs.

Guidelines for citing electronic sources are still in flux. The guidelines for electronic citations included in current MLA and APA style guides are not definitive, nor are they up-to-date. Phyllis Franklin, executive director of the Modern Language Association, explains the situation:

> We're not issuing definitive standards for usage. We expect standards to change as electronic communication becomes a standard factor in our lives. (*USA Today,* Wednesday, Feb. 2, 1995, 7D).

Since new areas of the Internet are created faster than guidelines can be written, you may need to adapt the guidelines given in this chapter to accommodate new kinds of electronic resources that don't exist as this book is being written.

If you publish your research paper on the Web, you will want to create hypertext links to your Web sources. In a Web research project, a "citation" includes a link to a Web source. Print sources are documented following traditional research paper guidelines. For examples of Web research projects, see "Online Courses and Student Work" (http://www.CWRL.UTEXAS.edu/online/index.html), a sampling of courses that require students to post their writing to the Web. Not all of these samples included Works Cited or References pages, but they probably should. The best way to add a Works Cited or References page to a hypertext research paper is to provide a link from the main page to a works cited page. See Daniel Anderson's hypertext essay "Not Maimed But Malted" (http://www.cwrl.utexas.edu/~cwrl/v1n1/article1/notmaimedbutmalted.html) for an example of how to document sources electronically.

General Guidelines

The rule of thumb for citing electronic sources is to include the following information:

author's name
title of the work
date of publication or creation of the information
online address
date the source was accessed

The guidelines for MLA and APA are presented in the sections that follow.

If the source you are citing exists in print format as well as electronic format, provide readers with the source information for the print material (including page numbers) before providing the Web source. For the Web source, provide the number of paragraphs in lieu of page numbers.

Note that in all cases, at the beginning of the entry (after the author's name), you need to indicate either the date the source was first published or the date it was last revised; at the end of the entry, provide the date that you accessed this source. The explanation for providing both publication date and date of access is simple: The version of the Web source that you saw may bear little resemblance to the way the site looks at the time someone reads your paper. By providing the dates, you indicate to your reader that you have tried to be as accurate as possible. You have no way of providing your reader with the exact Web source if that source has changed. For this reason, many college instructors request that you make hard copies of all Web pages that you cite.

Because most Internet users have access either to Netscape or to Lynx, URL addresses can be used in citation style to provide readers with methods for locating Internet sources.

MLA Electronic Citation Style

The *MLA Handbook for Writers of Research Papers,* fourth edition, treats electronic materials as if they were nothing more than extensions of print sources. Internet scholars thus tend to depart from the advice in the MLA Handbook, since it is already out-of-date.[1] The suggestions for MLA citation of electronic documents in this chapter are based largely on guidelines set forth in "Beyond the MLA Handbook: Documenting Electronic Sources on the Internet" [http://www.csc.eku.edu/honors/beyond-mla] by Andrew Harnack and Gene Kleppinger.

These Harnack and Kleppinger guidelines suggest a simple format for citing Web addresses: enclosing the URL in angle brackets (<>). Punctuation at the end of the citation is placed outside the brackets, thus avoiding the problem of having end-of-sentence punctuation mistakenly included in a Web address. For example, the Web site for this book would be referred to in this way:

Rodrigues, Dawn. *The Research Paper and the World Wide Web Online Guide.* October 9, 1996.
 <http://www.prenhall.com/rodrigues> (October 25, 1996).

---

[1] For details of the new MLA guidelines for electronic citation, see "Citing Electronic Materials with the New MLA Guidelines," by Michael N. Salda <http://www-dept.usm.edu/%7engdept/mla/rules.html.

Some guidelines recommend using Online followed by an Available statement. The alternate way of referring to the Web site for this book would be:

```
Rodrigues, Dawn. The Research Paper and the World Wide
     Web Online Guide. October 9, 1996. Online. Available
     World Wide Web. URL: http://www.prenhall.com/rodrigues
     (October 25, 1996).²
```

If the source you are citing is an online journal or newsletter, you need to indicate the pages or, if no pages are used, the number of paragraphs in the online document. In the Works Cited list for MLA style, you would indicate the total number of paragraphs or pages.

```
Noguera, Pedro. "A Popular Movement for Social Justice."
     (1996): 20 par. In Motion Magazine.
     <http://www.inmotionmagazine.com/pedro2.html>(April 12,
     1996).
```

In the in-text citation, you would need to indicate the specific page or paragraph in which your quotation appears, e.g., (Noguera, par. 3).

General Format for Web Addresses

```
Author. "Title of Document" Title of Complete Work. Date of
     publication or last revision. <Web address> any
     additional directions for retrieving source (access
     date).
```

Use the same general format for all Web addresses (http, Telnet, Gopher, and FTP). As indicated in the examples below, the URL or Web address is sufficient to provide availability information. Instead of providing a Gopher path for information at a Gopher site such as MARVEL, the Library of Congress Gopher site, you can provide the URL for the site. Readers who want to use a Gopher program rather than a Web browser to access this information have all the information they need. For example, a citation for a Gopher menu item called "News from the Center for the Book" would look like this in MLA style:

```
"News from the Center for the Book." September 26, 1996
     <gopher://marvel.loc.gov/00/loc/pubs/lcib/1996/
     vol55.no15/8> (October 20, 1996).
```

Citations for Web addresses would look like this:

```
Greenman, Ted. "Students Against Affirmative Action and for
     Equality." 29 Aug. 1996. <http://www.cwo.com/~tag/saaae.
     html>(17 Sept. 1996).
```

---

²Since all Internet sources are "available online," the terms seem redundant and are not suggested in the MLA guidelines as recommended in this book.

Brown, Haines. "Citations of Electronic Documents in an
     Electronic Document." <http://neal.ctstateu.
     edu/history/cite.html>(29 May 1996).
Gomes, Lee. "Xerox's On-Line Neighborhood: A Great Place to
     Visit." *Mercury News*. 3 May 1992.
     <telnet://lamba.parc.xerox.com 8888> @go #50827, press 13
     (5 Dec. 1994).

Photocopy the chart on page 164 to guide you in collecting information for citing Web, Telnet, or FTP sites.

General Format for Mailing List, Newsgroup, and E-mail Citations

Name of author. <Author's e-mail address> "Subject of
    Message." Date sent. <Address of list or UseNet group>
    (access date).

Use a similar format for mailing list, newsgroup, and e-mail citations. The author's e-mail address is included so that a reader can write to
the author and ask for a copy of the document. Some mailing lists keep
archives; others do not.

If the message you are citing is from an archived mailing list (a list
that stores past messages for later review and retrieval), you can include
the directions for accessing the archive.

Mailing List

Reiss, Donna. <dreiss@norfolk.infi.NET> "Moo Workshops" 9 Nov.
     1966. <acw-l@ttacs6.ttu.edu
Gardner, Traci. (traci!daedalus.com) "ACW-L Frequently Asked
     Questions." 5 June 1996. Archives: Alliance for Computers
     and Writing List (ACW-L). <http://www.ttu.edu/lists/acw-
     1/9606/0022.html> (20 Oct. 1996).

Newsgroup

Slade, Robert. <res@maths.bath.ac.uk> "UNIX Made Easy." 26
     Mar. 1996. <alt.books.reviews> (31 Mar. 1996).

E-mail

Lewis, Wayne D. <wdlewis@utb.edu> "Tif Proposal Deadline" 29
     Sep. 1996. Personal e-mail. (3 Oct. 1996).

WWW, Telnet, and FTP Addresses

AUTHOR	TITLE	TITLE OF COMPLETE PUBLICATION, IF APPLICABLE	DATE OF PUBLICATION OR LAST REVISION	HTTP: ADDRESS (INCLUDE ADDITIONAL DIRECTIONS, IF NEEDED)	DATE OF ACCESS

If you quote a message sent to you by someone else, make sure that you ask for permission. Also let the sender know that you have included his or her e-mail address in your Works Cited page.

Photocopy the chart on page 166 and use it to guide you as you collect information to cite mailing list, newsgroup, or e-mail sources.

General Format for Synchronous (Real-Time) Conversations

```
Name of author. Type of Conversation. <Web address> (access
    date).
Harnack, Andrew. Group Discussion. <Telnet:
    moo.du.org/port=8888> (4 Apr. 1996).
```

If the MOO conversation you are quoting is a personal one, indicate "Personal Conversation" in the citation.

General Format for CD-ROM and Database Citations

```
Author. "Title." Title of Print Publication. Date of
    publication. Title of Electronic Work. Edition.
    Information supplier. Information on how to access file,
    such as file identifier number. (access date)
Oxford English Dictionary Computer File: On Compact Disc. 2nd
    ed. CD-ROM. Oxford: Oxford UP, 1992.
```

Note: Access dates are not needed for CD-ROM citations if the CD-ROM is not revised regularly. Since there is no parallel print publication, you cite only the CD-ROM.

```
Banks, R. Richard. "Race Matters Most." Los Angeles Times. 22
    May, 1995, A5. Electric Library. <http://elibrary.com/>
    (17 April 1996).
```

Note that the page number for the online newspaper is included. The Electric Library database is accessible through the Web, thus the URL address for the database is all that you can provide to the reader. If a reader wishes to locate your source, he or she will have to search for the author and/or the title using the search engine in the database.

Use the chart on page 167 to enter your own CD-ROM or database information.

APA Electronic Citation Style

With a few exceptions, the APA style guidelines suggested in this chapter are based on Xia Li and Nancy Crane, *Electronic Style: An Expanded Guide to Citing Electronic Information* (1996), by Information Today, Inc.

Mailing List, Newsgroup, and E-mail Addresses

AUTHOR'S NAME OR LOGIN ID IF NAME IS NOT AVAILABLE	AUTHOR'S E-MAIL ADDRESS	SUBJECT OF MESSAGE	DATE MESSAGE SENT	ADDRESS OF LIST OR USENET GROUP	DATE MESSAGE WAS ACCESSED

Collecting CD-ROM and Online Databases

AUTHOR	TITLE OF WORK	TITLE OF COMPLETE PUBLICA- TION, IF APPLICABLE	DATE OF PUBLICA- TION OR LAST REVISION	TITLE OF ELECTRONIC WORK	MEDIUM	INFOR- MATION SUPPLIER (E.G., ERIC)	FILE ID OR HTTP ADDRESS	DATE OF ACCESS (IF REGULARLY REVISED)

APA style guidelines require that you provide a reader with exact access information. If you cannot provide readers with a way of retrieving the material you have cited, then you should provide the primary source in an appendix. If you want to quote from an informal MOO conversation, you can; but you do not include the source in your References list. If you think you might want to quote from a given MOO conversation, be sure to "log" or capture the conversation so that you will have a record of it if anyone asks to see the entire transcript. Check the software on your computer to see how it logs the results of an entire online session.

Although Li and Crane recommend using the term *Online* in an Internet citation, the guidelines that follow recommend merely indicating the Web address. Some readers will access these resources in different ways (Telnetting directly, using an FTP program, etc.); providing the URL seems sufficient, since it gives everyone the information needed to locate the resource. An example of Li and Crane's format and that recommended here will illustrate the differences.

Li and Crane recommend the following format:

```
Johnson, T. (1994, December 5). Indigenous people are now
more combative, organized. Miami Herald [Online], p. 29SA (22
paragraphs). Available:
gopher://americas.fiu.edu70/00/herald/herald.417 [1995, July
16].
```

The guidelines below, which omit "Online," recommend this format:

```
Johnson, T. (1994, December 5). Indigenous people are now
more combative, organized. Miami Herald, p. 29SA (22
paragraphs. Available: gopher://summit.fiu.edu/gopher://
americas.fiu.edu:70/00/herald/herald.417 [1995, July 16].
```

General Format

```
Author/editor. (Year). Title (edition), [Type of medium,
if not a Web source.] Producer or publisher (for proprietary
material). Availability information. [Access date].
```

If you are citing a Gopher, Web, Telnet, or FTP site, provide the URL immediately after the word Available (e.g., Available: http://www.pren hall/com/rodrigues). For CD-ROM databases [proprietary sources] or other electronic media, provide the producer or publisher and identifying information that would enable a reader to locate the material you accessed. Remember to provide an access date at the end of the citation.

General Format for Web Addresses

    Author/editor. (Year). *Title* (edition) and publication
information. Available: http:// or gopher:// or telnet://
[Access date].

If no publication date is available, write "No date." Use the same general format for all Web addresses (http, Telnet, Gopher, and FTP). End with the access date. Do not put a period after the address. If you are citing an online journal or newspaper, you should indicate the pages from which you have taken your quotation; in the References list, provide the number of paragraphs.

Web Addresses

    Li, X., & Crane, N. (1996). Bibliographic formats for
citing electronic information. Available:
http://www.uvm.edu/~xli/reference/estyles.html [1996, April
29].

    Greenman, T. (1996, August 29). Students against
affirmative action and for equality. Available:
http://www.cwo.com/~tag/saaae.html [1996, September 17].

    Johnson, T. (1994, December 5). Indigenous people are now
more combative, organized. *Miami Herald,* p. 29SA (22
paragraphs). Available: gopher://summit.fiu.edu/MiamiHerald--
Summit-Related Articles/12/05/95--Indigenous People Now More
Combative, Organized [1995, July 16].

    Noguera, P. (1996). A popular movement for social
justice. *In Motion Magazine* (20 paragraphs). Available:
http://www.inmotionmagazine.com/pedro2.html [1996, September
24].

    Rockwell, P. (1996, April 17). Angry white guys for
affirmative action. Available:
http://www.inmotionmagazine.com/rocka.html [1996, April 30].

    Sanchez, C. (1996, January 13) Future of affirmative
action in higher education. National Public Radio. *Electric
Library,* p.B5 (9 paragraphs). Available:
http://www.elibrary.com. [1996, October 1].

    Viviano, F. (1995, May/June). The new Mafia order. *Mother
Jones Magazine* (72 paragraphs). Available:
http://www.mojones.com/MOTHER_JONES/MJ95/viviano.html [1995,
July 17].

General Format for Mailing List, Newsgroup, and E-mail Citations

Use a similar format for mailing list, newsgroup, e-mail citations, and synchronous conversations, making slight adaptations as needed.

Mailing List or Newsgroup

```
Author. (Year, month, day). Subject of message.
Discussion List or Newsgroup [Type of medium]. Available:
[address or directions for retrieving from archive] [Access
date].
```
Slade, R. (1996, March 26) UNIX made easy. Available: news://alt.books.reviews [1996, March 31].

E-mail

```
Author (Sender's e-mail address). (Year, month day).
Subject of Message. E-mail to receiver's name. (Receiver's e-
mail address).
```
Rodrigues, D. (drodrigues@utb1.utb.edu). (1996, October 5) Ocean Creek Institute. E-mail to Susan Lang (slang@siu.edu).

Ask the sender for permission to quote a message sent to you. APA guidelines recommend that you give the e-mail addresses of the sender and the receiver. Let the sender know that you have included his or her e-mail address in your References list.

Synchronous (Real-Time) Conversations

```
Speaker. Type of Communication. [Access date].
```
Harnack, A. Group Discussion. Available: telnet://moo.du.org/port=8888 [1996, April 4].

General Format for CD-ROM and Database Citations

Many libraries have put their CD-ROM database collection online. In other cases, libraries subscribe to online databases for their campus. Someone who is not a registered student cannot use the privately owned databases. If the database is available on the Internet, even though it is available only to registered users, give the URL. If the database is available in another medium (e.g., CD-ROM), then indicate that medium.

```
Author. (Year, month day). Title. [edition and volume
number] [Type of medium], page cited and page numbers.
```

```
Available: Supplier/Database name (Database identifier or
access number) [Access date].
```

Oxford English dictionary computer file: On compact disc
(2nd ed.), [CD-ROM]. (1992). Available: Oxford UP [1995, May
27].

Goodwin, M. E. (1992). An obituary to affirmative action
and a call for self-reliance. (ERIC Document Reproduction
Service [CD-ROM], No. ED357998).

Goodwin, M.E. (1992). An obituary to affirmative action
and a call for self-reliance. (ERIC Document Reproduction
Service, No. ED357998) Available telnet://ERIC@sklib.
usask.ca:23/ (Log in as ERIC). [1996, October 22].

The ERIC Document Reproduction Service collections are available
in many different formats, including CD-ROMs and Web sites. The two
previous examples illustrate how you would cite either of the two ERIC
sources. Note that if you are citing an Internet source, the only indication
of the type of medium you are using is the presence of a URL.

Howell, V., & Carlton, B. (1993, August 29). Growing up
tough: New generation fights for its life: Inner-city youths
live by rule of vengeance. *Birmingham News* [CD-ROM], p. 1A (10
pp.). Available: 1994 SIRS/SIRS 1993 Youth/Volume 4/Article
56A [1995, July 16].

Suggestions for Citing Web Sources:

• Don't put any periods at the end of the URL.

• Examine URLs carefully so that you are sure you are copying them
correctly. If possible, copy the URL from the online source and paste
it into your notecards so that you don't misspell it.

• Note both the date the item was created and the access date (the
date you retrieved the source).

• If the Web source you are quoting is a journal, current guidelines
suggest that you include the number of paragraphs (just as, for a
printed source, you indicated the number of pages).

• Ask the author of an e-mail message for permission before you cite
it. Note: Although Li and Crane recommend including e-mail references, the trend in APA style is to treat e-mail as personal corre-
spondence, which in standard APA style is *not* included in the
References list, though it is noted in the in-text citation.

FORMATTING THE RESEARCH PAPER: MLA AND APA EXAMPLES

Different documentation styles also have different styles of page formatting. Most research papers do not require title pages, but if your instructor asks for one, follow our suggested format. A sample title page, abstract page, first page, and references page in APA style appear after the MLA research paper.

MLA STYLE FIRST PAGE WITHOUT A TITLE PAGE

MLA STYLE TITLE PAGE

CENTER TITLE

$^{1}/_{3}$ DOWN THE PAGE

The Importance of Affirmative Action

by

DOUBLE-SPACE

"BY" AND NAME

Ray Garcia

DOUBLE-SPACE

English 102, Section 1   COURSE, SECTION

Professor Wilson   NAME OF PROFESSOR

April 6, 1996   DATE

1"

MLA STYLE FIRST PAGE WITH A SEPARATE TITLE PAGE

Garcia 1

The Importance of Affirmative Action

INDENT ½"

At a recent "Day of Conversations" about diversity on my campus, I found myself disagreeing with both faculty and other students on affirmative action policies. This experience led me to realize that I needed to explore affirmative action in greater depth. I wanted to learn whether the lukewarm attitude toward affirmative action and diversity issues at my campus was symptomatic of national trends. What is the current status of affirmative action programs nationally? What is the attitude on other campuses toward affirmative action? And if affirmative action programs in their current form are in trouble, are there any viable alternatives for reducing discrimination and promoting diversity?

It may help to begin with some background about affirmative action. Affirmative action is a series of programs, put into place during the sixties, which were designed to make up for previous disadvantages that minorities as groups have had. The arguments in favor of affirmative action stress the need to remedy the effects of past discrimination against minorities and women. The ways of remedying prior discrimination include:

- special admissions programs;
- special scholarship programs; and
- changes in the curriculum (since according to some past curricula have been based on a white European bias

and, although often inadvertently, non-European cultures
have not been included in textbooks and courses).

President Lyndon Johnson issued Executive Order 11246
calling for "affirmative action" among federal contractors,
colleges, universities, and the federal government. It is a
means of increasing the numbers of minorities and women in
colleges, universities, and federal programs (qtd. in Lappe
97).

He explained the need for affirmative action in a June
1965 address at Howard University, noting that freedom of
opportunity doesn't immediately level the playing field.

> You do not take a man who for years has been hobbled
> by chains, liberate him, bring him to the starting
> line of a race, saying 'you are free to compete with
> all others,' and still justly believe you have been
> completely fair. Thus it is not enough to open the
> gates of opportunity. (qtd. in Lappe 97)

For more than two decades affirmative action programs
have been in place and, even though they haven't dramatically increased the numbers of minority students and faculty, they have helped. More importantly, they have helped
develop students' respect for diversity. A study done found
that students from all racial and ethnic groups showed
strong support for diversity efforts in the curriculum
(Lopez 33).

In spite of successes, there's been much disagreement
about affirmative action. Arthur Levin, President of Columbia Teachers College, said recently, "What we'll see in the
next few years . . . is that unless there's enormous pressure behind affirmative action it's going to fall off the
tray" (qtd. in Sanchez 32).

A series of court challenges has threatened affirmative action programs or seriously undermined them in many
colleges and universities. Jachik and Lederman report that
in March 1996, the United States Court of Appeals for the
fifth circuit, ruling on Hopwood v. Texas, ruled that the
University of Texas could not base preferential racial or
ethnic admissions upon a claim that the university was trying to remedy past societal discrimination. Before this
ruling, all colleges and universities were able to recruit
minority students using special affirmative action criteria. Schools could set up affirmative action programs even
if the school itself had not ever been accused of discrimination. As long as minorities had suffered from discriminatory policies in the state or region of the country,
individual institutions were able to help redress past
wrongs through their affirmative action programs.

Court rulings are not the only indication that affirmative action programs are in trouble. In recent years,
there's been an erosion of interest in affirmative action,
even by minorities themselves. Critics of affirmative
action have crafted many arguments against it. They point
out the following problems with affirmative action programs:

• Preferential treatment for minorities creates a different kind of prejudice and a new kind of discrimination—a
discrimination against white males (Rockwell). The weakened
economy in California, with fewer jobs in higher education
now available, has stimulated greater support for anti-
affirmative action initiatives. White males think they'll

have more chance for employment if minorities do not get
preferential treatment.

  • Affirmative action stigmatizes minorities who benefit from it. (Even those who may be qualified enough to be
hired or admitted without affirmative action are assumed to
have been hired because of their minority status and so
feel the stigma.)

  • Affirmative action ignores individual merit.

  • Affirmative action gives minorities excuses for not
trying harder (Goodwin).

  • Affirmative action doesn't really work well anyway.
(According to a study at the Tomas Rivera Center, the percentage of Latino faculty within the University of California system has increased only minimally since affirmative
action programs began in the sixties.)

  • Affirmative action benefits the most qualified and
privileged people from the disadvantaged groups, leaving
the others as they always were; it's the upper-middle-class
minorities who tend to get into college or get jobs that
affirmative action programs make available.

  • Some groups argue that affirmative action isn't
really needed in some parts of the country. One group of
students at the University of California (Students Against
Affirmative Action and for Equality) has argued that diversity would exist on their campus without what they see as
offensive "racially based guidelines," since they live in a
place with a mix of cultures (Greenman).

  For all these reasons, affirmative action has been
losing supporters. As R. Richard Banks argues, there is an

increasing reluctance of intellectuals and politicians to identify social problems as explicitly racial problems. The only arguments that have gained some momentum are those that suggest that perhaps class rather than race should be used as the main criteria for preference in college and on the job.

Two key alternatives to affirmative action as we know it have been proposed. The first alternative suggests addressing inequity by looking at socioeconomic class rather than race. The second, responding to the anti-affirmative action sentiment in the country, is an even bolder maneuver—favoring no one, but having as a goal a diverse and multitalented student body. Both alternatives are described below.

Richard Kahlenberg offers a choice of several ways to address class rather than race in college admissions, ranging from a simple reporting of family income to a more complex series of calculations based on factors such as the neighborhood where a student lives, the quality of the high school that he or she may have attended, and family income. His argument is based on the research that shows that lower socioeconomic class blacks have not seen any real benefit of affirmative action.

Suggesting that preferential treatment might best be determined by economic need, two white male professors placed an anti-affirmative action initiative on the ballot. They feel that a class-based affirmative action system would preserve the goals of affirmative action, but be fairer to everyone. Feeling strongly that poor students should be helped, Jack Kemp suggests a new role for affirmative action, that of "ending the educational monopoly that makes poor public school students into pawns of the educational bureaucracy."

Not everyone agrees that it would be better to base affirmative action on class rather than race. Some note that poor whites outnumber the poor of other races. Further, whites and Asians tend to score higher on SAT tests, so socioeconomically poor whites and Asians might benefit disproportionately more than poor blacks, Hispanics and American Indians if class rather than race were the criteria for designating recipients of affirmative action awards (Dickerson).

Banks feels that both race and class have to be factored in, even though race matters more. In "Race Matters More," he maintains that proposals to base affirmative action on economic class alone rather than on race ignore fundamental truths about the interplay of race and class (32). Banks feels that if we really cared about helping others, we'd come up with ways of factoring both race and class into affirmative action programs. His point is that it is illogical to think that helping poor people equates with helping black people. He sees the whole attempt to focus on class alone as a way of skirting the real issue—an inability to "confront the depth of our racial difficulties." (320) He notes that blacks who are poor have difficulty competing in society not only because of their poverty but also because of their color. He does not think that "remediating class disparities will dissolve our racial difficulties . . ." (33).

The second alternative to affirmative action programs as they have been traditionally practiced has been started by the University of Texas-Austin, a highly selective school. Instead of using SAT scores and allowing a certain number of students who fall below the score to qualify because of race, the administration has announced a new policy: all applicants will be reviewed individually. Subjective criteria including such items as family background and responses to written essays will be reviewed by a committee that will make admissions recommendations (University of Texas C7). Using this system, race should still be allowable as a factor of putting together a mix of students that will constitute a heterogeneous freshman class. This system was prompted by the fact that too many high-scoring students apply for admission to UT Austin. An admissions policy based on numerical scores would fill all available slots at the school, leaving no room for students of color who have much potential that does not show up on scores alone. The proposed new policy is similar to practices used by Ivy League institutions and elite private schools.

Clearly, the affirmative action issue is a tricky one and resolving it will not please everyone. Preserving the notion of affirmative action through having some class-based programs along with revised admissions policies may help. But just as important as these programs is continuing to work on the prejudicial and discriminatory mindset that many individuals have grown up with. If affirmative action based on race is replaced by either of the suggested

alternatives, there is no guarantee that general efforts to
foster multiethnic and multiracial understandings will stay
in place on campus.

The real issue is deeper than the arguments over
affirmative action seem to imply. The key problem is the
racial issue itself. Affirmative action programs have been
a way of addressing discrimination. Along with providing
minorities access to an education, affirmative action programs have other purposes. In particular, they are designed
to foster so-called "diversity" on campus, including diversity in the curriculum.[1] These programs need to be kept
alive.

Unfortunately, universities seem particularly apa-
thetic. Perhaps a key reason that there's been little alarm
and worry is that schools have too many other problems
right now. A report on interviews with various administrators indicated that universities and colleges may very
easily not contest the challenges for they currently have
other serious issues to address, such as budget problems
and loss of credibility among their constituencies. As
Claudio Sanchez put it, "The end of affirmative action in
the University of California system . . . has exposed some
deep-seated misgivings about racial preferences in hiring
and admissions . . ." (NPR interview).

---

[1]Diversity is a term used to refer to the value of
having people from diverse backgrounds and cultures
together on campus. Diversity efforts on campus are geared
to reducing prejudice and to promoting an understanding of
different cultures. Often diversity programs support multi-
cultural programming on campus and promote curricular
changes that reflect the ethnic background of students on a
given campus.

What will happen if nothing is done to preserve at least the diversity initiatives related to affirmative action? As Pedro Noguera points out, "Without a policy that holds universities and employers accountable for who they admit, the pledge to not discriminate is meaningless" (50). People who have grown up with prejudicial attitudes toward other groups do not change their belief systems easily. Without some programs to bring minorities and other poor into college, society will lose.

Columnist Bill Bradley is convinced that racism and discrimination won't go away easily because "many people hold values that allow them to defend the social advantage they have based on being upper-class whites" (10). Unfortunately, Bradley's observations seem accurate.

Affirmative action has helped lessen discrimination and prejudice, but it has taken more than 20 years to begin to see benefits from the gains of affirmative action programs. Looking at the gains of minority enrollment in colleges is telling: "National enrollment figures illustrate that enrollment of people of color has grown from negligible figures when schools were segregated to about 20% of the nation's post-secondary education students" (Lappe 47). That pattern won't continue if affirmative action programs end.

What can be done? As Goodwin notes, what blacks needed then, and need today, is equalization of resources and facilities, not just affirmative action policies. He calls for a new political vision that "asks people to engage each other" (2).

I think that colleges should help stimulate this engagement in issues. Instead of letting affirmative action dominate the conversation, colleges should encourage students from all racial backgrounds to interact more with one another. They also should encourage more substantive discussion of the issues. Only by exploring diversity issues in depth do the complexities emerge.

The bottom line is this: college administrators, faculty, and students know that racial issues and tensions have not been solved by affirmative action programs. Affirmative action programs as we know them are not likely to survive. It is up to individuals who care to keep multiethnic concerns alive. Individual students, professors, and administrators can and must make diversity on campus a continuing concern. It is up to individual students' and professors' minds and hearts. Special programs such as the "Days of Conversations" held on our campus must continue, with improved formats that keep the conversations going after the day is over.

MLA STYLE—WORKS CITED LIST

Works Cited

Alicea, I. P. "Dismantling Affirmative Action." *Journal of Blacks in Higher Education* 5.19 (1995): 4.

Banks, R. Richard. "Race Matters Most." *Los Angeles Times* 22 May 1995: A5. *Electric Library* <http://www.elibrary.com/> (17 April 1996).

Bradley, Bill. "Ending Racism Can Never Be Just About Numbers." *Los Angeles Times* 15 Jan. 1996: B5. *Electric Library* <http://elibrary.com/>. (17 Sep.1996).

Dickerson, M. "Affirmative Action Opponents: Class-Based Help Would Do More." Gannett News Service 1 April 1995: 10 par.) <http://elibrary.com/> (10 Aug. 1996).

Goodwin, M. E. "An Obituary to Affirmative Action and a Call for Self-Reliance." ERIC Document Reproduction Service. CD-ROM. No. ED357998, 1992.

Greenman, Ted. "Students Against Affirmative Action and for Equality." 29 August 1996. <http://www.cwo.com/~tag/saaae.html> (17 Sep. 1996).

Jachik, S., and Lederman, D. "Appeals Court Bars Racial Preference in College Admissions," *Chronicle of Higher Education* 42 (1995): 26-29.

Kahlenberg, Richard. "Class, Not Race." *New Republic* 3 Apr. 1995: 21-27.

Kemp, Jack. "Affirmative Action: The 'Radical Republican' Example." *Post* [Cincinnati] 24 Aug. 1995: PG. *Electric Library* <http://www.elibrary.com/> (10 Sep. 1996).

Lappe, Frances Moore. *Rediscovering America's Values.* New York: Ballantine Books, 1989.

Lopez, Gretchen E. "Beyond Zero-Sum Diversity: Student Support for Educational Equity." *Educational Record* 76.1 (1995): 55-62. ERIC Document Reproduction Service. CD-ROM. No. EJ 508623. (1 Oct. 1996).

Noguera, Pedro. "A Popular Movement for Social Justice." *In Motion Magazine.* (1996): 20 par. <http://www.inmotionmagazine.com/pedro2.html> (12 Apr. 1996).

Rockwell, Paul. "Angry White Guys for Affirmative Action." 17 April 1996: 11 par. <http://www.inmotionmagazine.com/rocka.html>. (30 Apr. 1996)

Sanchez, Claudio. "Future of Affirmative Action in Higher Education." National Public Radio. 13 January 1996: 9 par. *Electric Library,* p. B5 <http://elibrary.com>. (1 Oct. 1996)

"University of Texas Drops Automatic Admissions Policy," *Valley Morning Star* 9 June 1996: C7.

APA STYLE TITLE PAGE

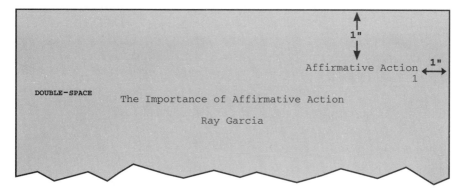

1"

Affirmative Action

1"

1

DOUBLE-SPACE   The Importance of Affirmative Action

Ray Garcia

APA STYLE ABSTRACT PAGE

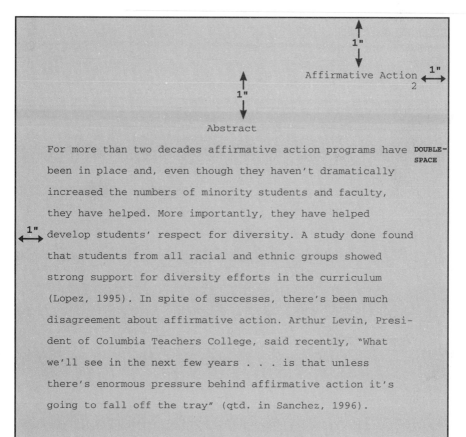

1"

Affirmative Action

1"

2

1"

Abstract

For more than two decades affirmative action programs have   DOUBLE-SPACE

been in place and, even though they haven't dramatically

increased the numbers of minority students and faculty,

they have helped. More importantly, they have helped

1"   develop students' respect for diversity. A study done found

that students from all racial and ethnic groups showed

strong support for diversity efforts in the curriculum

(Lopez, 1995). In spite of successes, there's been much

disagreement about affirmative action. Arthur Levin, Presi-

dent of Columbia Teachers College, said recently, "What

we'll see in the next few years . . . is that unless

there's enormous pressure behind affirmative action it's

going to fall off the tray" (qtd. in Sanchez, 1996).

APA STYLE FIRST PAGE

Affirmative Action
⟵ 1" ⟶
3

1"

DOUBLE-SPACE   The Importance of Affirmative Action

At a recent "Day of Conversations" about diversity on
my campus, I found myself disagreeing with both faculty and
other students on affirmative action policies. This experience led me to realize that I needed to explore affirmative
action in greater depth. I wanted to learn whether the
1"
⟵⟶ lukewarm attitude toward affirmative action and diversity
issues at my campus was symptomatic of national trends.
This paper will explore the status of affirmative action
programs nationally, examine some alternatives to such programs, and suggest ways for preserving the essence of
affirmative action--the reduction of discrimination and
racism in society.

It may help to begin with some background about affirmative action. Affirmative action is a series of programs,
put into place during the sixties, which were designed to
make up for previous disadvantages that minorities as
groups have had. The arguments in favor of affirmative
action stress the need to remedy the effects of past discrimination against minorities and women. The ways of remedying prior discrimination include:

• special admissions programs;

• special scholarship programs; and

• changes in the curriculum (since according to some

DOUBLE-SPACE

APA STYLE—REFERENCES LIST

References

Alicea, I. P.(1995). Dismantling affirmative action. *Journal of Blacks in Higher Education* 5 (19), p. 4.

Banks, R. R. Race matters most. (1995, May 22). *The Los Angeles Times*, p. A5 (22 paragraphs). *Electric Library.* Available: http://www.elibrary.com [1996, April 17].

Bradley, B. (1996, January 15). Ending racism can never be just about numbers. *The Los Angeles Times*, p. B5 (9 paragraphs) *Electric Library.* Available: http://www. elibrary.com. [1996, September 17].

Dickerson, M. (1995, April 1). Affirmative action opponents: Class-based help would do more. Gannett News Service. (10 paragraphs). [1996, August 10].

Goodwin, M. E. (1992). An obituary to affirmative action and a call for self-reliance. [CD-ROM] (ERIC Document Reproduction Service, No. ED357998).

Greenman, T. (1996, August 29). Students against affirmative action and for equality. Available: http://www.cwo.com/~tag/saaae.html [1996, September 17].

Jachik, S., & Lederman, D. (1995). Appeals court bars racial preference in college admissions, *Chronicle of Higher Education, 42,* 26–29.

Kahlenberg, R. (1995, April 3). Class, not race. *The New Republic,* pp. 21–27.

Kemp, J. (1995). Affirmative action: The "radical Republican" example. *The Post* (Cincinnati), 08-24-1995, p. PG. *Electric Library.* Available: http://www.elibrary.com [1996, September 10].

Lappe, F. M. (1989). *Rediscovering America's values.* New York: Ballantine Books.

Lopez, G. E. (1995). Beyond zero-sum diversity: Student support for educational equity. *Educational Record, 76*(1), 55–62. ERIC Document Reproduction Service. [CD-ROM]. No. EJ 508623. [1996, October 1].

Noguera, P. (1996). A popular movement for social justice. *In Motion Magazine* (20 paragraphs). Available: http://www.inmotionmagazine.com/pedro2.html [1996, September 24].

Rockwell, P. (1996, April 17). Angry white guys for affirmative action. Available: http://www. inmotionmagazine.com/rocka.html [1996, April 30].

Sanchez, C. (1996, January 13). Future of affirmative action in higher education. National Public Radio. *Electric Library*, p. B5 (9 paragraphs). Available: http://www. elibrary.com [1996, October 1].

"University of Texas drops automatic admissions policy," *Valley Morning Star* (Hailinger, TX) 1996, June 9: C7.

EXPLORING CITATION PROBLEMS

The Web poses new problems for researchers. As you know if you've visited the same Web site several times, the content can change, sometimes daily. In the past, someone who wanted to check the sources in a research paper could access the very same source that the writer used. With the Web, it's almost impossible to be sure that your reader will have access to the identical information you have.

There are other problems, too. The addresses for sites change. It may be that when your readers type in the URL that you provided in a research paper they will get a message indicating that there is no known URL with that address.

Another problem is a logistical one. It isn't easy to keep track of URLs. Some browsers don't show the URL of the page you are viewing. Most sites do not include the URL on the page itself. Thus, if you save a Web page to disc thinking that you've got your information intact, you may discover later that you don't have the URL. It's easy to do a Web search on your topic and find the URL—far easier than running back to the library and taking a book out again—but it is a problem that you can avoid if you are careful. Here are some suggestions:

- Save the file with the name of the URL.
- Open files as soon as you save them and copy the URL into them.
- If you print pages immediately rather than save them to disc, check to see if Netscape now automatically prints the title of the file. Netscape places the URL in the header of each page.

Here is a general form you might use to keep track of online sources you plan to cite in your paper:

AUTHOR	DATE	TITLE	AVAILABILITY	ACCESS

PRACTICE BOX

1. Discuss the importance of being able to track down a specific site. Do some teachers and scholars pay excessive attention to tracking sources? Consider the following example of how an author uses excessive detail in a citation: Why is it so important, in this person's opinion, to have all the detail?

Vail, E. <Esther.Vail@p15.f333.n2613.z1.fidonet.org>, Reynolds, L. <vog@rain.org>, and Taibi, Solomon <taibi@ix.netcom.com>. 'Middle Names Part II'. Articles <814840481.AA00152@rochgte.fidonet.org>, <46s2sl$k55@news.rain.org>, <46s70l$8tf@ixnews4.ix.netcom. com> and <46t4m5$2jp@crl10.crl.com>, in: USENET newsgroup alt.usage.english

The author of this citation explains her view:

It is possible to omit them [the long codes for articles] considering the ephemeral nature of news articles. However, bear in mind that it is already sometimes possible, and will in the future be increasingly so, to look up articles in news archives (see, for example, <http://www.dejanews.com>), so it is usually better to include them.

2. There is considerable difference of opinion among scholars as to the format of electronic sources. Melvin Page, a history professor, believes that URLs should begin on a new line so that the text can be easily converted to HTML documents. Should citation format vary so much from one discipline to another?

3. Gather a list of sources for a project you are working on. With a partner, write them in correct electronic citation format. In small groups, review your work. As you begin writing citations for Web sources, you'll discover many difficulties, since Web resources are so varied. In all likelihood, you'll find that you have to "create" ways of citing some of your sources. See if you can come to some agreement on the most appropriate way to format your citations.

COPYRIGHT CONSIDERATIONS

In addition to knowing how to document sources, you need to understand copyright laws. The term "copyright" refers to protection provided to authors for their "copy"—whether a printed text, a movie, a visual, or a recording. From 1989 on, copyright protection has been automatic, and a simple statement such as "this document cannot be distributed in its entirety without permission of the author" is all that you have to do to guarantee your authorial rights. Also, include a copyright symbol (©) and the date. (Such a statement is not absolutely necessary but it can prevent accidental misuse by others.)

Before the Web, students rarely had to worry about copyright laws. The few lines of text from books or journals that are included in student papers are within the "fair use" length guidelines. (You can quote up to 300 words from a book or 150 words from a magazine or newspaper, if the total you quote is not more than 20% of the original.) But if you link a source on the Web to your text, you can be considered to be "distributing" that source. It is always advisable to get permission to link to a given site. Most importantly, if you are writing a hypertext research paper that includes links to copyright-protected essays or poems that you have photocopied and included in an Appendix to your research project, don't scan the text into the computer and link it to your writing without receiving permission from the author. If you do, you may be guilty of copyright infringement.

CONCLUSION

Citation conventions for print-based sources have been set in place for years; Internet citation style, however, is still evolving. When you use the Web for research, you should continue using the same processes for citing sources that you've always used; but it *is* essential that these processes be adapted to Internet-specific needs of readers. Clearly, it is not always easy or even possible for a reader of an Internet-based research paper to track a source. But it is important that you, as a writer, do your best to provide clear and accurate guidelines for your readers.

If you have some doubts, include an explanatory footnote in which you let your reader know the context: for example, you may find that a given source that you found at a specific Web site is no longer there. If that is the case, use the source if you feel it is critical to your point, but be honest with your reader.

Above all, continue using the Internet for research. Don't let concerns about validity and citation questions stop you from including the results of your Internet-based research into your finished paper.

END-OF-CHAPTER EXERCISES

1. Discuss issues involved in Web citation. What if you want to include a citation in a bibliography but have never actually visited the site? Should you access the site? Do you always take a book out of the library just so that you can list it in a bibliography? (Note the discrepancy.)

2. When is it important to know the date the site was developed and/or last modified? Historian Melville Page explains that to him, the important date is the date the information was developed, not the date it was last modified. He sees a difference between technologists and historians. Do you feel it is important to give both dates?

SUGGESTIONS FOR RESEARCH AND WRITING

A current collection of sources related to these topics can be found at the Web site for this book.

1. Examine several Web sites that include recommendations on Internet citation style. Do a paper on the relative importance of following correct citation style. You might conduct an Internet survey to determine whether some schools and students take documentation guidelines less seriously than others.

2. Explore the nature of citation style and convention in different disciplines. Here are some questions to guide your investigation: Why are citations so important? Why do some disciplines (for example, the sciences) use Citation Indexes? How do citations conventions emerge? Are these conventions necessary? Are Internet citation guides available for different disciplines? In your report, summarize the citation styles recommended for at least four different disciplines.

3. Do authors follow citation style? Do an investigative report on the extent to which student and professional research papers follow the documentation styles suggested in this chapter. You might interview students in different majors on your campus; you might find the names of random students at schools across the country and ask them whether their professors expect them to adhere to documentation style. Be sure to look at sample papers posted on the Web, too.

GLOSSARY

Bandwidth   Term of measurement for width of Internet cables. Wider bandwidths allow more data to pass through them.

Bauds per second (bps)   The rate at which data passes through a modem.

Bibliographic Records   A record is a set of information that is stored as a unit. A bibliographic record contains publication information.

Boolean searching   Searching that is based on the logical principles set forth by mathematician George Boole. If you want to find many sources on your topic, you can use two synonyms for your topic combined with OR (e.g., technology OR distance education). If you want to limit the number of sources you find, you should use AND. (Technology AND distance education would result in only those sources that use both terms.)

Browser   A software program designed to allow users to explore the World Wide Web.

Cataloging software   Software used to organize a library's holdings.

CD-ROM   Storage medium for computer data.

Chat areas   Web or other Internet sites where individuals "chat" by typing messages to one another. Chat areas are usually focused on a specific topic.

Database   Software designed to allow a user to enter information into categories in such a way that it can be sorted and retrieved at a later date.

Descriptors   Keywords from the text of an article used when storing information in a database or when retrieving information.

Digital age   Term used to refer to the information age or age of technology as opposed to the age of print or the age of books.

Digitize   To turn a picture or a printed page into a computer format that allows the data to be transformed.

Digitized photographs   Photographs that have been put on disk and that can be resized or edited.

Directory   Groups of files stored together. Similar to folders and sub-folders in Macintosh and Windows environments.

Disc   Sometimes spelled disk or diskette, this term usually refers to a floppy disk (either 5¼" or 3½").

Domain suffix   The domain is the place where your Internet service originates. The suffix is the end portion of an Internet address that indicates the nature of your site. For example, **edu** indicates an educational site, whereas **gov** indicates a unit of government.

Download   Term used for the procedure of moving information from a remote computer to your own computer.

E-journals   Articles collected together on Internet sites. Sometimes these journals are "refereed" (sent out to reviewers in the field before acceptance). Web journals are typically done in hypertext format.

E-mail   Method of communicating with others by sending messages from one computer address to another.

E-mail address   The unique set of letters followed by a computer's location name that is provided to you so that you can send and receive messages across the Internet.

Electronic sources   Sources that are in nonprint media.

Eudora   E-mail program available in Macintosh or IBM-compatible versions.

Folder   Metaphor for an area on a computer where individual files (and other folders) are stored.

FTP   File transfer protocol. The standard way of getting files from a remote computer and putting them on your computer or of putting files from your computer on the remote machine.

Gopher   Menu-based software designed to interact with other computers running similar software.

Gopher interface   The screen design or way of enabling users to access information on the Gopher system. Gopher uses a treelike system to organize information into files and folders.

Graphical interface   A computer screen display that enables a user to point and click to select information and navigate the program. On the Web, it is a way of providing access to information through pages that are designed with attractive text and images, some portions of which are linked to other Web pages through hypertext links.

Hit   A match between a search term and a word in one of the titles or texts that are in the database.

Home page   The starting "page" or the first screen in a set of Web pages.

Each home page has links to many other pages either at the current site or at other locations.

HTML   Hypertext Markup Language—the way of coding text, images, and other digitized files to make them accessible through the Web.

HTTP   Hypertext Transfer Protocol—the set of standards for transmitting data on the Web.

Hypertext   Text that includes links to other text or images, usually accessible by clicking on underlined words or phrases in the initial document.

Images   Pictures or drawings that have been digitized and stored on a computer.

Information resources   Computer-accessible books, journals, pictures, audio files, etc., that can be retrieved via the Internet.

Interactive forums   Discussion or chat software accessible through Web sites. Messages are stored for easy reading and responding.

Interface   The part of the computer screen design that suggests ways of navigating the program.

Internet   World-wide network of networks, including Gopher sites, Web sites, and FTP sites.

Keywords   Words related to a given topic used to locate information on that topic in a database.

Launch   Term used to start an application such as Telnet or FTP.

List server   Computer used to administer and organize mailing lists. Two popular mailing list programs that run on list servers are Listproc and LISTSERV.

Location box   Place in the Netscape screen which displays the address of the Internet site currently being viewed.

Login or Log in   When you log in to a computer you identify yourself to the computer so that it can check to see if you are an authorized user. Typically, you need both a **login name** and a **password** to identify yourself with a computer.

Login name   The set of letters and/or numbers used to identify yourself to the computer. This name is often used as part of your e-mail address.

Login Prompt   Typically, the word "login:" which appears on the screen of a computer that requires an access code, as a way of "prompting" you or reminding you of what you need to do next. In this case, a login prompt indicates that you need to enter your **login name** and press <Enter>.

Lynx   A text-based Web browser that runs on the UNIX operating system. To use Lynx, you typically need to have access to a UNIX computer at your campus or workplace. DOS versions of Lynx are also available, but not common.

Main menu   The opening list of selections on a given program.

Menu   A list of selections that appears on the opening screen of a program or on a subsection of a program.

Modem   Device used to translate computer data into a format that can be sent through standard telephone lines. Modem stands for modulator-demodulator.

Netscape   Graphical browser that integrates newsgroups, mail, FTP, Gopher, and Web access into a common program.

Newsgroup   Discussion groups on various topics, accessible through a browser or through special software called newsreaders or through Internet sites that provide public access to newsgroups.

Online   Term used to refer to information available on the Internet.

Online source   A source that can be accessed on the Internet.

Operators   Terms used to describe AND, OR, and NOT when used to separate keywords in a search. Each of these terms directs the way the search "operates." Also called Boolean operators. See *Boolean searching.*

Packets   Clusters of computer data that are coded at transmission and decoded at the destination.

Password   Secret way of identifying yourself to a computer on which you have an account. The **login name** is the public way you identify yourself to the computer.

Path   The location of files is frequently referred to by giving its "path" or place in a **directory** structure. For example, if a file named "book.txt" is stored in a subdirectory of a directory called "pub," its path would be /pub/book.txt. Longer paths indicate deeper directory and subdirectory structures.

Post   To send a message on e-mail to a mailing list or to a newsgroup.

PPP   Point-to-point protocol (agreed-on standard). Method of transferring Internet data from one point to another.

Query   To request information by inserting search terms into a database.

Records   Sets of information stored in a database.

Remote site   Any place away from the location of your computer. If you can log in to your computer from another location, then you are said to have remote access.

Screen   The visual information that appears on your computer monitor. Depending on the size of the computer monitor, a screen can hold less than a page or several pages of text.

Search engine   Computer program designed to look through massive amounts of information in a database and retrieve a list of resources that match your **query.**

Search form   The area on the search tool where you enter the **keyword**s and other information needed to perform a search.

Search screen   The image that appears on your computer when you indicate to a **search tool** that you would like to perform a search.

Search tool   Computer program used for searching a database, sometimes including various categories of information that can be searched along with a **search engine.**

Service provider   A company that provides Internet "service" or access.

Shell   A program allowing limited access to a UNIX computer.

Site   Computer location that offers specific directories and subdirectories of information accessible through Internet browsers or through such programs as **Gopher** or **FTP.**

Source code   The set of commands that tell your browser how to display a page on your computer screen.

Supercomputers   Extremely powerful computers used primarily by scientists and often shared with others who log in from remote sites.

Surfing   Term used to describe the act of moving rapidly from site to site on the Web.

Telnet   Term coined from the words "telephone" and "network." Telnet software enables you to use phone lines or other Internet lines to log in to computers at other sites around the world, provided that you have a **login name** and a **password.**

Terminal   A monitor and keyboard that interacts with another computer. When you **log in** to computers at remote sites, your computer becomes nothing more than a terminal or transfer device for viewing or interacting with information on the remote computer.

Text-based interface   A computer screen display that requires a user to type commands rather than use a mouse to point and click to select actions. When you Telnet to an Internet site (such as a library), you are in a text-based environment rather than a graphical one.

Transfer files   To move files from one computer to another, usually using software such as Xmodem or Kermit.

Uniform Resource Locator   The URL or address for an Internet site.

URL   Uniform Resource Locator or address for an Internet site.

Usenet   Bulletin board system designed in the 1970s by computer scientists, which is now used for newsgroups or discussion groups by individuals everywhere.

WAIS   Wide Area Information System—a software package that enables multiple databases at remote sites to be searched using the same query system.

Web interface   A way of accessing information through the graphical kind of screen typical of the Web.

Web page   Units of information one or more screens in length, but often no longer than one or two pages. Web pages are linked together with anchors that allow you to jump from one to the other.

Web site   Location of a computer called a server that contains the home pages for your company, department, or group.

World Wide Web   That portion of the Internet that has been formatted with hypertext links. These links can be text files, audio files, graphic images, or video.

Z39.50   Protocol used by librarians to organize and code their catalog information in such a way that allows it to be searched with a common **search form.**

Zine   Term coined from maga*zine* to refer to the many collections of essays or samples of creative writing that are made available on the Internet.

Works Cited

Day, Michael. "Writing in the Matrix: Students Tapping the Living Database on the Computer Network." in *The Dialogic Classroom* by Galin and Latchaw. NCTE: Urbana, IL, in press.

Dobler, Bruce and Harry Bloomberg. "How Much Web Would a Web Course Weave if a Web Course Would Weave Webs?" in *The Dialogic Classroom* by Galin and Latchaw. NCTE: Urbana, IL, in press.

Franklin, Phyllis. "Footnotes in the Electronic Age," *USA Today* 6 February 1996: D7.

Galin, Jeff and Joan Latchaw. *The Dialogic Classroom*. NCTE: Urbana, IL, in press.

Jacobson, Robert L. "Researchers Temper their Ambitions for Digital Libraries," *The Chronicle of Higher Education* 24 Nov. 1995: A19.

Jones, Steven G., ed. *Cybersociety: Computer Mediated Communication and Community*. Sage: Thousand Oaks, CA, 1995.

Kling, Ron and Lisa Covi. "Special Issue on Electronic Journals and Legitimate Media in the Systems of Scholarly Publishing." *The Information Society,* <http://www.ics.uci.edu/~kling/klingej2.html> 10 October 1996.

Macrorie, Ken. *Searching Writing*. Rochelle Park, NJ: Hayden. 1980.

Smock, Raymond W. "What Promise does the Internet Hold for Scholars?" *The Chronicle of Higher Education,* 22 Sept. 1995: B1.

Tennant, Roy, "The Best Tools for Searching the Internet," *Syllabus* 9:5 (1996) 36–38.

Zimmerman, Don and Dawn Rodrigues. *Researching and Writing in the Disciplines*. Harcourt, Brace, Jovanovich: New York, 1993.

Index